Water, Water Everywhere
Paean to a Vanishing Resource

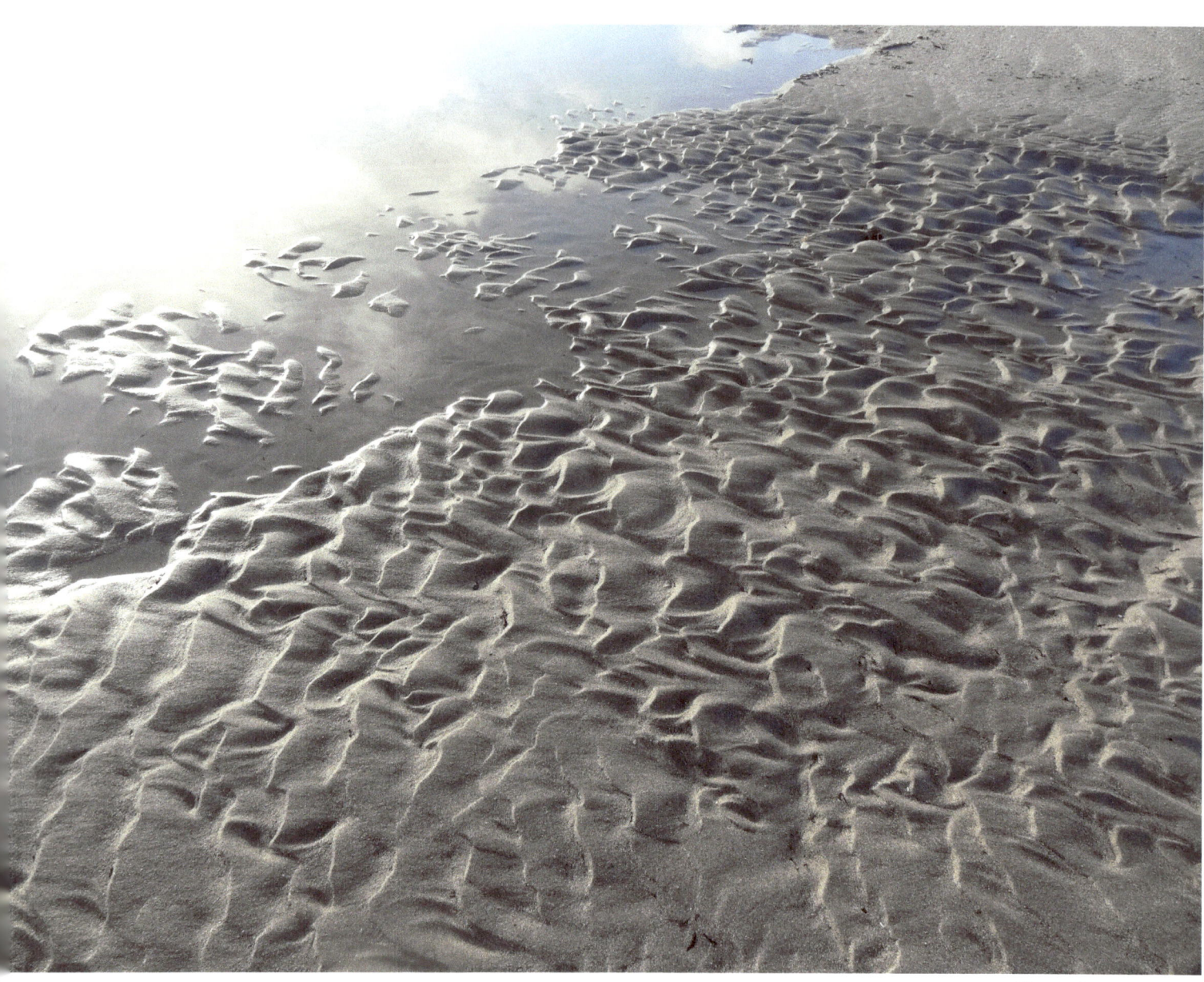

Photo by Shireen Malik, 2012.

Water, Water Everywhere
Paean to a Vanishing Resource

Curated by Jennifer Heath

Foreword by Ismail Serageldin

©Jennifer Heath, 2014

Cover photos ©Shireen Malik, 2012

"Water is Life," © Ismail Serageldin, 2014

"Remembering the Source," © Betsy Damon, 2014

Designed by Sweet Design

No part of this book may be reproduced without permission of the writers and the artists.

All rights reserved.

baksun books & arts
for Social & Environmental Justice
1838 Pine Street
Boulder, Colorado 80302 USA

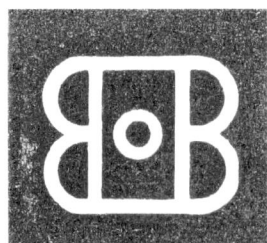

ISBN 1-887997-30-X

In memory of Peter Warshall

Ecologist, activist, essayist, and friend of poets

Water, Water Everywhere:
Paean to a Vanishing Resource

is funded in part by

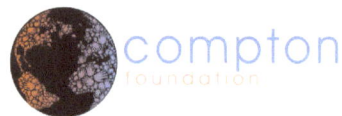

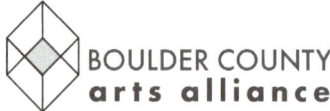

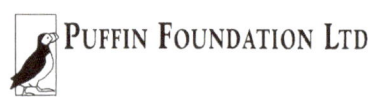

and

with special thanks to

J. Gluckstern

Shireen Malik
www.shireenmalik.com

Jack Collom

Lucy R. Lippard

Valerie Behiery

Felicia Furman

Katie Hyzy

Rickie Solinger

Claudia Borgna
ClaudiaBorgna.com

Kathy Maria Marsh
www.facebook.com/pages/Irishartnow/145306362157643
www.irishartnow.com/KATHY-MARSH

Sarah C. Bell

Heather Sarbaugh

Marda Kirn
www.ecoartsonline.org

Ashraf Zahedi

Table of Contents

Foreword: Water is Life
    Ismail Serageldin 2

Water, Water Everywhere:
    Lamentations, Celebrations, and Healing Songs
    Jennifer Heath 5

Remembering the Source
    Betsy Damon 19

Currents and Divides 23

The Artists 73

Exhibition Checklist 86

Resources 87

Questions About Water 90

FOREWORD

Water is Life
Ismail Serageldin

Water is life. Without water we die. In fact without water we would not be here at all. While most people know this truth, they don't realize just how much water we need to survive. Most people think of drinking water as the key. But if we take some 2-3 liters to drink per day, and maybe consume another 15 for flushing waste, and 10 for cooking and 15 for a bath and invest 40 or 50 liters in energy and industry to support the economic activities that give us the goods and services we need, that is still nothing. Indeed, the average person consumes some 2,500 liters of water every day, which is what it takes to produce 2,500 calories of the food we eat. Roughly 1 liter per calorie!

Although about three-quarters of the surface of our blue planet is covered in water, and up to about 95 percent of the volume of livable space is water, that water is salt water. Freshwater is only 2.5 percent of that total. And of that, about two-thirds is locked in glaciers and ice-caps, currently threatened by rising global temperatures. Thus our freshwater resources are very precious indeed. Furthermore, renewable freshwater resources are unevenly distributed. Canada and the Northeastern United States have approximately 10,000 cubic meters of freshwater per person per year, whereas Jordan has less than 100! Rainwater comes in concentrated bursts in particular seasons and locations, resulting in many floods and droughts.

Underground water in aquifers is being drained faster than the recharge rates, which results in declining water tables almost everywhere. And our water consumption as persons and societies continues to grow. In the last century, Earth's population trebled, but water consumption increased six fold.

Few natural river basins are located within the borders of a single country. More than 270 rivers are shared by two or more countries, calling for cooperation rather than competition in basin management. Alas, such cooperation is the exception rather than the rule.

Although most societies and religions have a spiritual bond to water, whether in ritual or in concept, we continue to misuse and abuse our water resources. We continue to mismanage water both at the national and the individual levels. In most countries at least six and sometimes as many as twenty different government agencies are responsible for regulating different aspects of water, the largest consumer being irrigation for agriculture. But water is

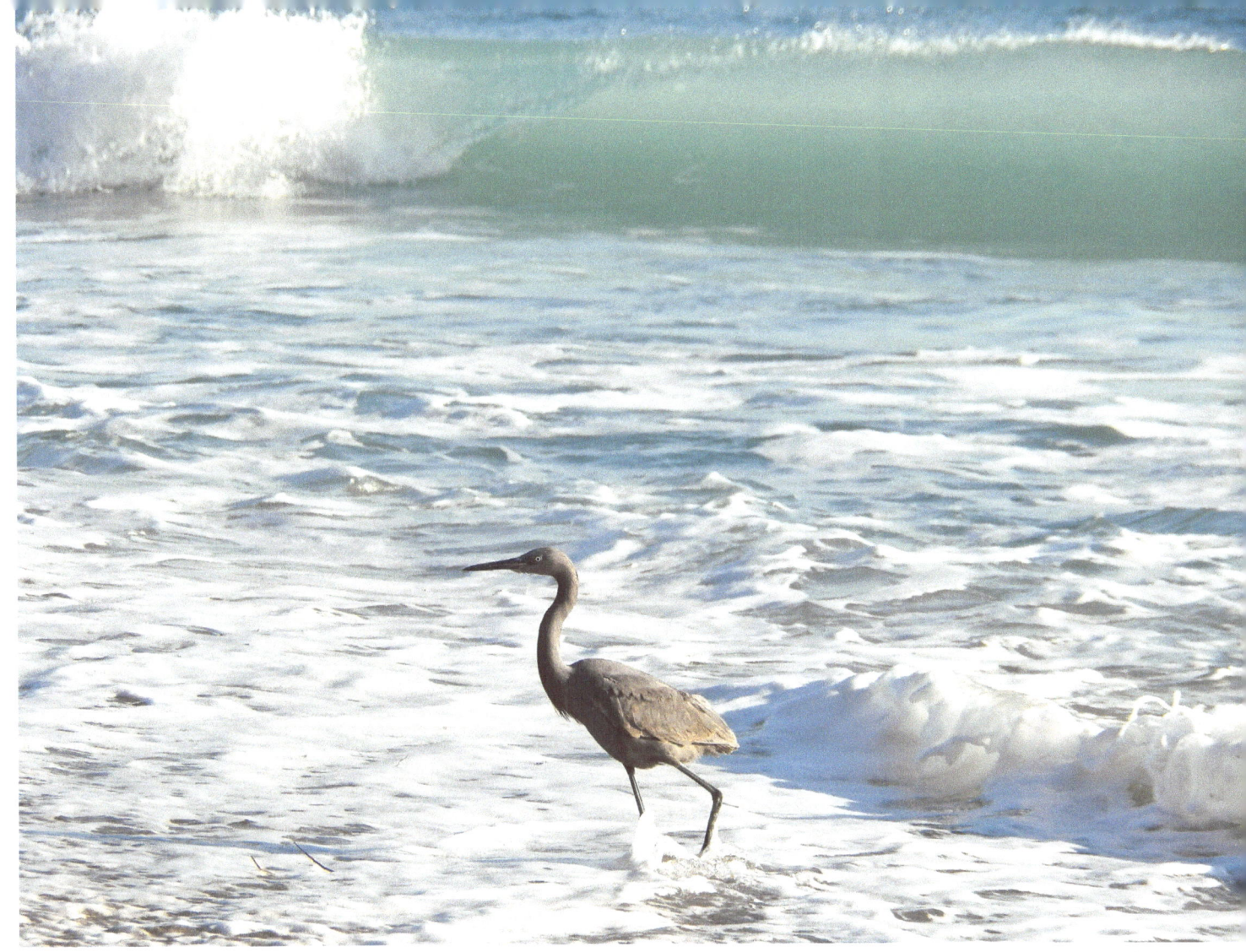

Photo by Shireen Malik, 2012.

also essential for industry and energy, as well as for municipal and household use. It is equally important for navigation, leisure, and to maintain the environment. Wetlands, which we have devastated in the last century, play an important role in the balance of the hydrological cycle of Nature.

And all this addresses only the quantity aspect of water. The quality aspect is equally important. Pollution and contamination of water affect the manner in which it can be safely used, and put strain on Nature to recycle it. Even the oceans, vast as they are, are not immune from human damage as we witness rising acidification. And what is more, climate change is reducing glaciers and ice caps and affecting the pattern of rainfall, the fundamental source of surface freshwater that we rely on.

It is not just the scientists and environmentalists who are concerned with water. Water also speaks to the artists in our midst, and they in turn tell us about it in their own inimitable ways. The sea with its millennial appeal to those who would brave its storms to find new shores, the serenity of a lake and the life-giving force of a river, the beauty and grandeur of snow and ice, the lush jungles that water makes possible, and the beautiful beaches which we enjoy... all attract humans in many different ways. The beauty of water and its universal appeal is undeniable, and the many strange and beautiful life forms that live beneath its surface call out to our curiosity and our interest. From coral reefs – those magnificent magical gardens that are habitats for extraordinary biodiversity – to the microscopic world in a single drop of a pond, water is teeming with life. And we are the custodians of that life.

Against this background, *Water, Water Everywhere: Paean to a Vanishing Resource* is a remarkable, interactive traveling multi-media exhibition intended to raise awareness about these important issues. It is a privilege to write this brief foreword for the catalogue of this noteworthy effort. May it travel far and wide, and engage people everywhere in the magnificent realm of water, the realm of life.

Ismail Serageldin *is the Founding Director of the Bibliotheca Alexandrina, the new Library of Alexandria, Egypt, inaugurated in 2002. He serves as chair or member of numerous advisory committees for academic, research, scientific, and international institutions, as well as civil society efforts, including the Advisory Committee of the World Social Science Report for 2013 and the UNESCO-supported World Water Scenarios (2013-). He is also chair of the Executive Council of the World Digital Library (2010-), the Executive Council of the Encyclopedia of Life (2010-), and the ICANN Panel for the review of the Internet future (2013-) He has co-chaired the African Union's high-level Panels for Biotechnology (2006) and for Science, Technology, and Innovation (2012-2013). He was a member of the high-level group for the Alliance of Civilizations convened by the Secretary General of the United Nations (2006-2007). From 1992 to 2000, he was vice president of the World Bank and Chairman Consultative for the Group on International Agricultural Research (1994-2000). He is founder and former chairman of the Global Water Partnership (1996-2000) and the Consultative Group to Assist the Poorest (1995-2000). In addition, he has taught at the Collège de France, Paris, and was a distinguished professor at Wageningen University in the Netherlands. He has received the Japanese Order of the Rising Sun, the French Legion d'Honneur, is a Commandeur of Arts and Letters of the French Republic, and has been honored with Chile's Pablo Neruda Medal, India's Bajaj Prize for upholding Gandhian values outside India, was the first recipient of the Grameen Prize for lifelong efforts to fight poverty, and received the "Champion of Youth" award from the World Youth Congress in Canada. He has published more than sixty books and monographs and over 200 papers on topics ranging from biotechnology and rural development to sustainability and the value of science to society.*

Water, Water Everywhere
Lamentations, Celebrations, and Healing Songs

Jennifer Heath

I began writing this introduction to *Water, Water Everywhere: Paean to a Vanishing Resource* on the cold January day in 2014 that beloved folksinger Pete Seeger died. His passing may seem tangent to a catalogue about a touring new-media art exhibition, but Seeger, in addition to being a world-renowned musician and social activist, was a strong environmentalist, who, in 1969, with his wife Toshi and a few friends, founded Hudson River Sloop Clearwater, a group dedicated to cleaning the mighty watercourse that feeds New York and New Jersey. They approached the project with a creative and unusual idea, which some were convinced was folly. They built a boat, a majestic replica of the sloops that sailed the Hudson in the 18th and 19th centuries. Clearwater has succeeded by bringing people to the river where they can experience its wonders, form a relationship with it, and thus be moved to preserve it. Initiating the process of saving the Hudson River is thought by many to be Seeger's greatest legacy.

In 1972, Seeger and the Clearwater crew sailed the sloop to Washington, D.C., while Congress debated the Clean Water Act. Seeger personally delivered a petition and held a spontaneous concert in the Capitol Building. The Federal Water Pollution Control Act was soon passed despite then-President Richard Nixon's veto.

Alas, today the vast majority of polluters escape unpunished, as state officials repeatedly ignore obvious illegal dumping. It is not only human beings who are affected, but Nature as a whole suffers, too. The Environmental Protection Agency, which can prosecute polluters when states fail to act, often declines to intervene.

Two weeks before Seeger's passing, in early January, the Elk River, its surrounding lands, and the main water plant near Charleston, West Virginia, were poisoned by a chemical spill from Freedom Industries, which had not been inspected since 1991. No one can predict what future horrors may result from the spill.

Two months before Elk River, in November 2013, Typhoon Haiyan, thought to be the most powerful cyclone ever to make landfall, hit the Philippines, killing thousands and wiping out homes, land, potable water, food sources, and wildlife.

> "At best [artists] can make the hot breath of climate change both vivid and immediate to this visually oriented society. They can also deconstruct the ways we are manipulated by the powers that be and help open our eyes to what we must do to resist and survive."
>
> – Lucy R. Lippard

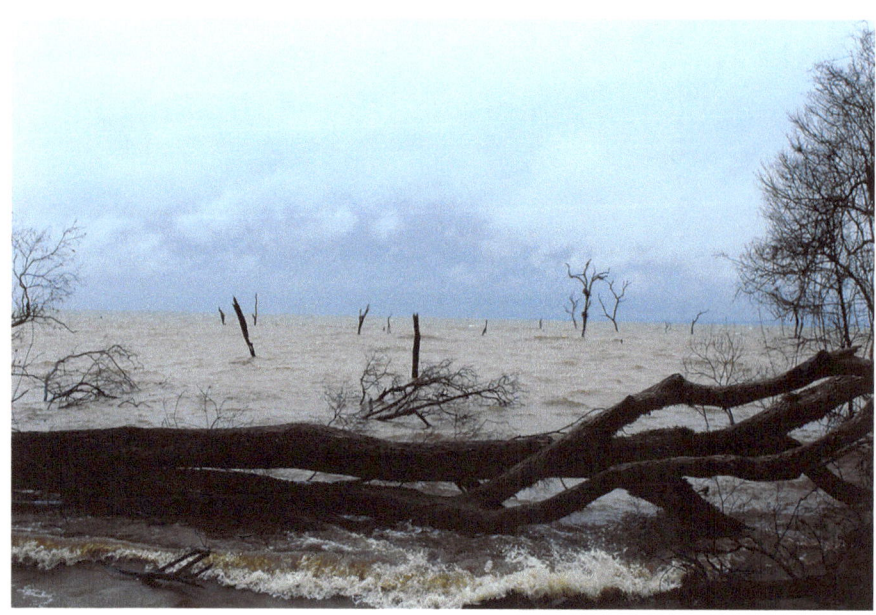

Carla Pataky and International Rivers, Inc., still from *A River Runs Through Us*, 2010.

Two years before Typhoon Haiyan, in 2011, the Tohoku earthquake and tsunami hit Japan, wrecking the Fukushima Daiichi power plant, which caused the largest nuclear incident since the Chernobyl disaster in 1986.

These are mere samplings of major water-connected upheavals in recent years. The catastrophic beat goes on: floods, droughts, pollution...

Water is the world's most crucial and precious resource, the basis for all earthly life. Its preservation and protection is our greatest environmental challenge and for that reason, I conceived this touring exhibition. I'm far from alone in my desperate concern about climate change, but producing and curating art exhibitions is the best way I know to respond. The call to care for Earth's water is growing louder and more distressed from artists, activists, progressive politicians, environmentalists, scientists, and many others – even the Pentagon – who understand the disastrous consequences if determined steps aren't taken planet wide ... soon. The global water challenge affects everyone, not just those unfortunately located in high-risk areas. Indeed, as we in so-called developed nations ignore the warnings – with overuse (sucking up watersheds and aquifers), toxins, dams, fossil fuel exploration, industrial agriculture, water privatization, and more – we are actually cultivating hazards that are bound to bounce back with deadly consequences.

Water, Water Everywhere is a touring exhibition that is the opening salvo of a planned climate-change trilogy, differing art projects whose common denominator is water. *Water, Water Everywhere* is comprised of 30-second to 30-minute films and videos from forty-five artists worldwide, who explore water issues from the political to the personal and from ethics to aesthetics, with works that are documentary, experimental, educational, humorous, solemn, animated, or acted. In our modern age, we too often see the natural world as mechanical and unresponsive, but these artists illuminate how we glance at or relate to, revere or neglect, use or misuse this element that is not only alive but essential to life. I find moving pictures exquisitely suited to illustrating water's myriad rhythms, melodies, behavior, and physical characteristics.

My intention was to create a flexible exhibit that could be presented in a variety of ways: as a water film festival; as a new-media gallery exhibition with video installations (there are as many possibilities for display as can be imagined: projections on walls, floors, building exteriors, pond surfaces...); and/or accompanied by two- and three-dimensional work by local artists addressing regional water issues. *Water, Water Everywhere* hosts can choose to show each of the films and videos individually or they can screen four pre-programmed disks (choreographed with the extraordinary filmmaker J. Gluckstern), titled "We're All Downstream," "Our Cup Runneth...," "Every Drop a World," and "A Commons. A Public Trust. A Human Right." These organize the exhibition's themes and arrange it aesthetically. Ruben Aubrecht's looped video, *april*, of rain slapping relentlessly against glass, is the exhibit's marquee piece, intended to be screened in an old-fashioned TV monitor, reminding us how television has become our window to Nature.

Regardless of how hosts choose to display it, *Water, Water Everywhere* is designed first and foremost to be a platform and inspiration for community discussions, panels, and individual talks, co-curricular activities, collaborations with scientists, environmentalists, activists, and artists, with activities and events that will bring light to the world water crises and the sanctity of water and its sources, as well as the beauty and strangeness of water.

Artists provide fresh perspectives and new insights into how we perceive our damaged world. Not every artist I chose for *Water, Water Everywhere* is devoted to making work about climate change and its assorted calamities, but water is so basic to every aspect of our being that many have simply used it as a dance of life's energy. Although most of the following descriptions derive from their statements, a few of the artists might be surprised at how I envisioned their individual films and videos fitting into the whole.

We're All Downstream

The bleak humor of Fiammetta De Michele's *Louisiana* features a scratchy recording of Tchaikovsky's *Swan Lake*. Odette, having been turned into a swan by an evil sorcerer, is now additionally cursed as her lake transforms into muck. The feathered dancer flails in sticky goo, slips repeatedly until she finally collapses, stuck in tar – an oil-saturated bird.

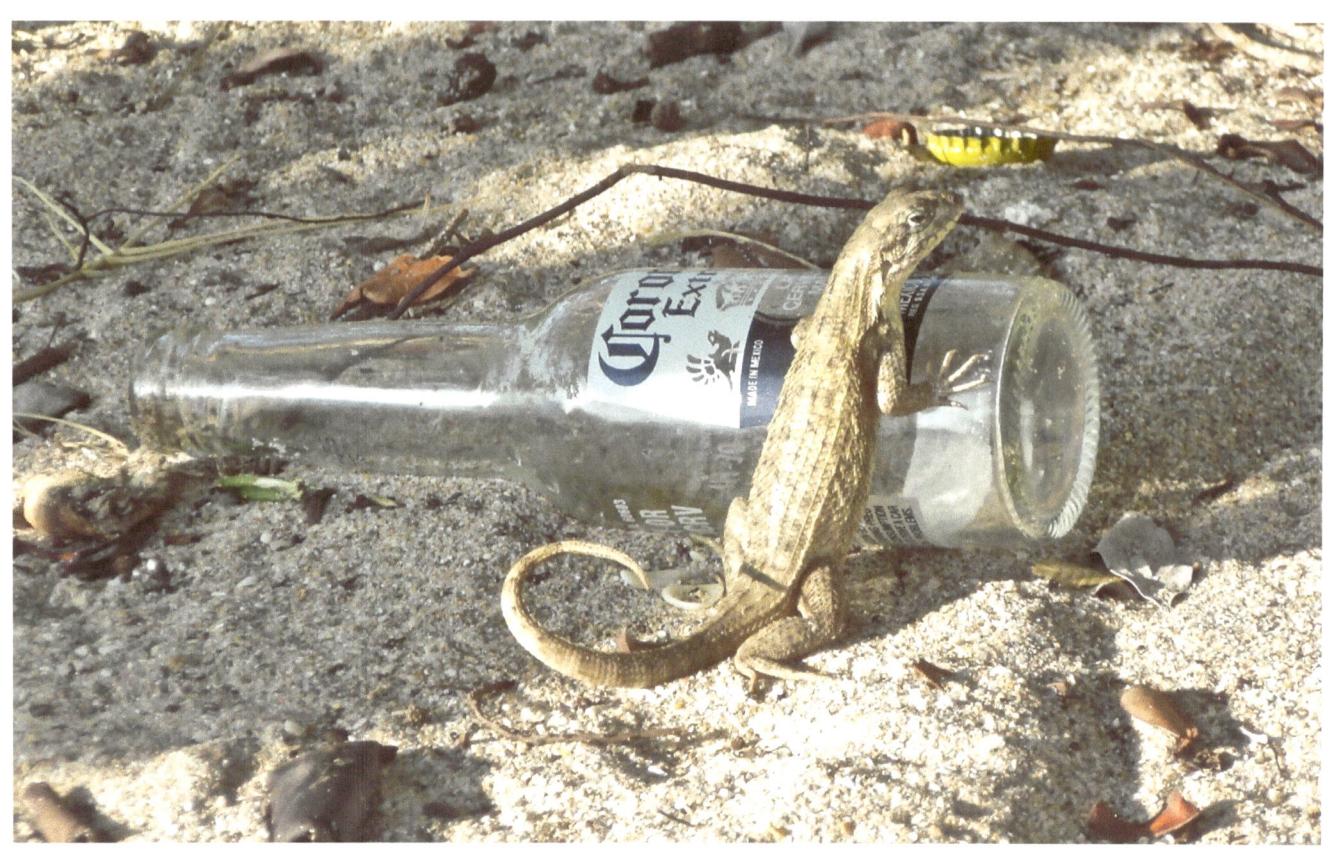

Photo by Shireen Malik, 2012.

Louisiana is a prelude to Michel Varisco's *Shifting,* which looks more pragmatically at the unique but fragile and deteriorating Louisiana wetlands before, during, and after the 2010 Deepwater Horizon – aka, British Petroleum – spill in the Gulf of Mexico, one of the worst environmental disasters in United States history. Drawing on art and science, in this gorgeous photo montage, Varisco stimulates discussion about conservation, use, and energy issues, offering her viewers a gentle, firm, essential lesson.

James Brady's *Floodland Study #1 – visible measures* evokes the primal grace of the Oglet shore salt marsh in the Mersey Estuary near Liverpool, England, as the artist accompanies a geographer and his students conducting paleo-environmental mud-core research. The artist does not try to explain the process, but instead gives us a mysterious, almost tactile experience of ancient soil, while the wild wind describes the shapeless passage of time … if only human beings understood time. As the poet Jack Collom has written,

> Nature's too slow
> people get
> bored.[1]

A River Runs Through Us documents a 2010 gathering in rural Mexico of activists from around the world, who comprise the growing global movement to protect rivers and their surrounding ecology from the ravages of big dams, which block fish runs, prevent essential sediments from reaching estuaries, and divert water from small communities to large agricultural concerns and urban areas. Dams unbalance the environment at all levels and have disrupted millennia of sustainable irrigation. Historian Steven Mithen writes that

> The need for management of the water supply has never been greater and is getting more serious by the day. The statistics ... are horrendous: one billion people – a seventh of the global population – do not have access to safe drinking water. Two billion people have inadequate sanitation. By 2025, more than half the world's nations will face shortages of fresh water; this is predicted to [rise] to 75 percent of the global population by 2050.[2]

Dams are not the answer. They – and other kinds of water management throughout history – are often undertaken for the self-aggrandizement of the powerful. Mithen reminds us that "we need the hindsight of history." For example, the history of the Hoover Dam "is as much about the political infighting and commercial competition, the quest to build personal reputations and gain financial success, as it is about the mechanics of tunneling through rock to create spillways and pouring concrete to create the dam."[3] And neither personal power nor cement is sustainable.

In her lively performance video, *Poise of Tides*, Claudia Borgna wades into a lake, collecting water in plastic bags. Borgna's artwork focusses on plastic bags, one of the most ubiquitous contaminations of Earth's environment. She turns them into landscapes, tools, sculptures that will, as plastic, last forever, though they seem so delicate. She is, in her own words, exploring "the contradictions of a neurotic world where creation and destruction co-exist.... Plastic bags epitomize the quintessential discarded object, a symbolic vessel wandering the landscape."

J. Gluckstern's *Ditches of Boulder* examines the extensive history of the irrigation system in a Colorado town, which could stand in for many towns in the

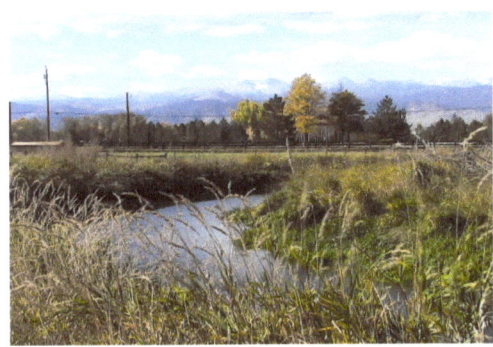
J. Gluckstern, still from *Ditches of Boulder*, 2009.

Ruben Aubrecht, still from *april*, 2005.

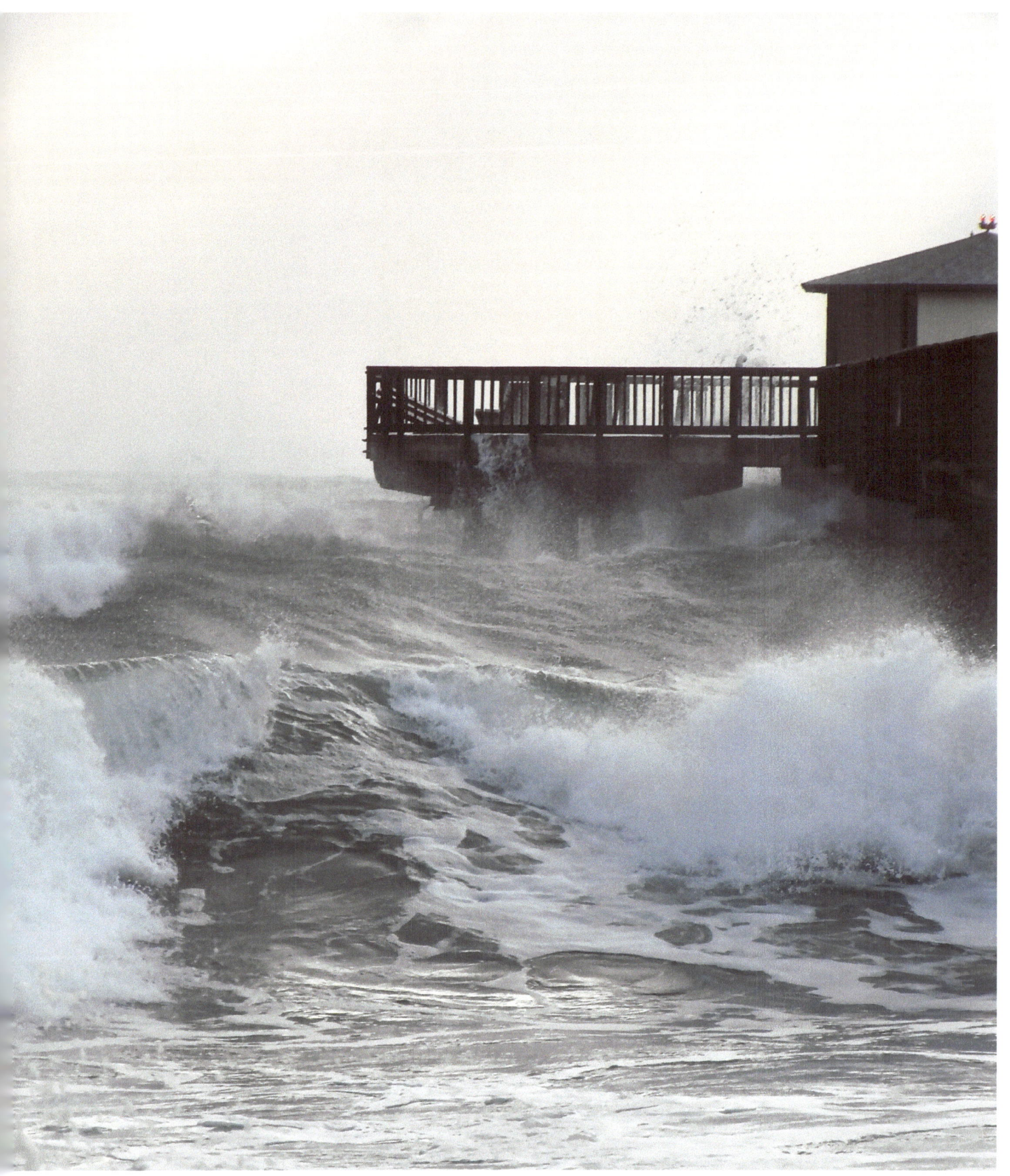

Photo by Shireen Malik, 2012.

U.S. West where water is scarce and growing scarcer.

In Gazelle Samizay's *im/pure*, unsullied water slowly fragments and distorts the pristine reflection of a woman – an expression both of emotions conjured by water and of water's susceptibility.

Indeed, water is susceptible to all manner of abuses, and among the worst is the process called hydraulic fracturing – "fracking" – taking place throughout the U.S. as the gas industry keeps profit margins high at any cost, while alternative forms of energy are ignored. Jacques del Conte's *A Colossal Fracking Mess* describes the destruction in Northeast Pennsylvania, as land, water, and livelihoods are wrecked by false promises of prosperity.

Susanne Wiegner's delightful animation, *Constant Dripping or No Escape*, pokes serious fun at our careless daily waste of water, while Jason Houston's *Indonesian Borneo: Water Meditation* – created during a project exploring the issue of deforestation in the critical habitat of endangered Bornean orangutans – offers 30 seconds of profound stillness, a welcome opportunity for contemplation.

Our Cup Runneth...

Basia Irland's *Book of Drought* is her memorial to water, a lament for the loss of crops, unsafe drinking water, insufficient levels for power generation, and the growing numbers of climate refugees. The UN estimates that by 2030, more than half the world's population will live in water-scarce areas. Meanwhile Samizay returns with *Left*, a poignant moment in which the performer seems to be sorting out, shard by shard, the aridity of a life without the sustenance given to us by water.

Äsa Maria Bengtsson and Ewa Cederstam's *FLOW* was shot in New Zealand and Greenland, situated on opposite sides of Earth. On one side, steam is the vital element, on the other, it is ice and frozen seas. The adjustments that those who live in such extremes must make seem implausible, but they also speak to astonishing human flexibility and Earth's marvelous multiplicity.

I Came...I Saw...Prayed for Someone Whom I Love, by Manoj Baviskar, mourns the decimated forests. The performer is painted blue, like the skin of Hindu gods, symbolizing peace and infinite space. The performer's hair and beard are shaved while trees are stripped by heavy logging equipment – a rape of Nature, an insult to the god's all-pervasive spirit.

Jaap Blonk offers *Flababble 1*, a humorous, slow-motion performance in which vigorous head shaking produces a sound not unlike splashing water, the soggy music of the human body, which is, after all, 70 percent water.

Christine Baeumler offers us two short pieces, *Surfacing* – which lovingly observes dolphins playing along the Great Barrier Reef – and *Amazon Twilight* – sunset, leading us into a fecund night sparkling with fireflies, stars, and lightning, accompanied by choirs of insects, birds, and frogs.

One Plastic Beach, by Eric Slatkin and Tess Thackara, documents San Francisco Bay Area artists, Judith Selby and Richard Lang, who have been collecting plastic debris from a single California beach for more than a decade. They sort and file, then create sculptures, prints, jewelry, and installations with their "treasures," helping to raise consciousness about plastic pollution in our oceans. This brings to mind the dreadful North Pacific Gyre, the largest ecosystem on Earth and the site of a massive collection of man-made marine debris, known as the Great Pacific Garbage Patch.

In *Sweep & Weep, Weep & Sweep,* Borgna's plastic bags are transformed into brooms. Propped upright, they could be flailing wind generators or otherworldly flora. Borgna's attempts to sweep the water recall Lewis Carroll's poem, "The Walrus and the Carpenter," referring to endless beach sand:

> "If seven maids with seven mops
> Swept it for half a year,
> Do you suppose," the Walrus said,
> "That they could get it clear?"
> "I doubt it," said the Carpenter,
> And shed a bitter tear." [4]

The poem and Borgna's performance are further sardonic reminders of the impossible debris left by humankind.

In the pleasurable, tranquil, multiple-frame *Sevastopol in August,* Tobias Rosenberger honors Leo Tolstoy's poetic *The Sevastopol Sketches:* "The sun was shining high and brilliant above the bay, which glittered warmly and cheerfully, studded with motionless ships and moving sailboats and skiffs…."

Diego Fiori's performance considers our mythic relationship with water in the award-winning *Silenzio: Birth and Death of the Alter Ego.* Life begins in water, and water is a primary element in the emergence tales of peoples everywhere. In mythology, folklore, and fairy-tale, water contains the gods, brings the dead back to life, cures illness, is a path to the otherworld, even bestows eternal youth.

Diane Armitage offers a moment of literal reflection with *The Great River,* as diamonds and stars bounce off the moving green waters of New Mexico's Rio Grande. From this festive salutation to water's beauty, Krisanne Baker's sol-

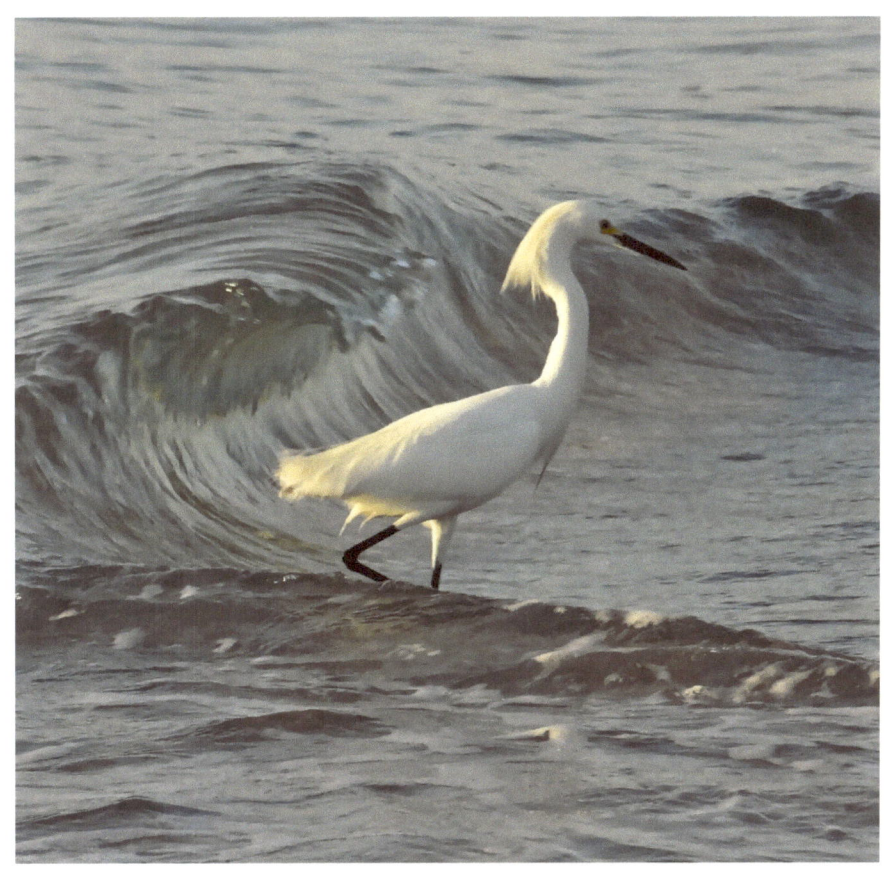

Photo by Shireen Malik, 2012.

emn *World Water Crises: Potential Effects/Cumulative Effects* shows us how quickly our good water is disappearing; how once it was considered a commons shared by all; how today it is subject to complex politics and alarming threats of privatization.

A Commons. A Public Trust. A Human Right.

In Robert Ladislas Derr's witty *Conservation of Momentum*, a man and woman spit water back and forth, defying gravity as water streams through space in a linear path. The artist expresses his wish that communication would "flow so seamlessly."

Conversation – communication – about our mutual resources is the crux of Irland's *A Gathering of the Waters*, a five-year performance that connected hundreds of culturally diverse people along more than a thousand miles of the Rio Grande/Rio Bravo, as the artist researched and marked its disparate path.

Carolyn Radlo and Alanna Simone open their stop-action *Rice Relief* with the sound of running water and washing dishes. Grains of rice twist and swirl in arabesques overlaid with snippets of conversation about food, aid, war, weapons, and need. The rice dances, the water splashes heedlessly down the drain.

In many places worldwide, the poor must purchase their water from private providers, paying prices that are as much as twelve times as high as water from municipal supply systems, so that the poorest among us pay the most.[5]

Good Water Neighbors, from Friends of the Earth Middle East/Palestine-Jordan-Israel, is an award-winning teaching documentary to raise awareness of the area's shared water problems. It aims to identify cross-border communities and develop dialogue about the shared dependence on water. Unfortunately, while the techniques used by *Good Water Neighbors* go a long way toward real improvement in water conservation and awareness, as well as toward building trust and peace, growing population points to dangerous overuse in what is currently the world's most water-scarce region.

With *Upstream, Downstream (In Our Bloodstreams)*, Baker reminds us of the unfathomable amounts of pollutants and DNA-altering chemicals we dump into our streams and rivers. Our waters are not only polluted by oil spills, but by arsenic, cyanide, and other toxins, as well as about fifty more chemicals that have been shown to have adverse effects on the development of fetuses and young children, as they mimic hormones and potentially interfere with the endocrine system and sexual development.[6]

Big Trash, by Monika Hapsari, addresses, through the voices of a mother and her four-year-old child, the awful misuse of irrigation ditches in Java used for the disposal of everything from household products to animal feces. The population is growing; government and community are apparently indifferent.

Tade (Impediment) by Smriti Mehra serves up another tragic irony. Traditionally, at the Indian Festival of Ganesh Chaturthi, the elephant-god idol was made of earth then returned to the Earth by immersing it in a body of water, an expression of the cycles of creation and dissolution in Nature. Increasingly, the idol is made of plastic and no longer dissolves. Ganesha, who is worshipped as the remover of obstacles, has become one himself.

Mary Rachel Fanning has used an underwater surveillance camera to create *The Trophy*, in which she monitors the hushed, lyrical motion of aquatic wildlife (and the occasional female swimmer). The camera was developed by fishermen, and in the artist's hands, moves across two frames between habitat and the hunt.

Henry Gwiazda explores similarities between shape and flow of earth and water and the relationship of sound to image in *there's whispering*, which leads us into a kind of birth sensation as land rises, flushed and fed by nurturing waters – all things connected in the *oikos*, the Earth household.

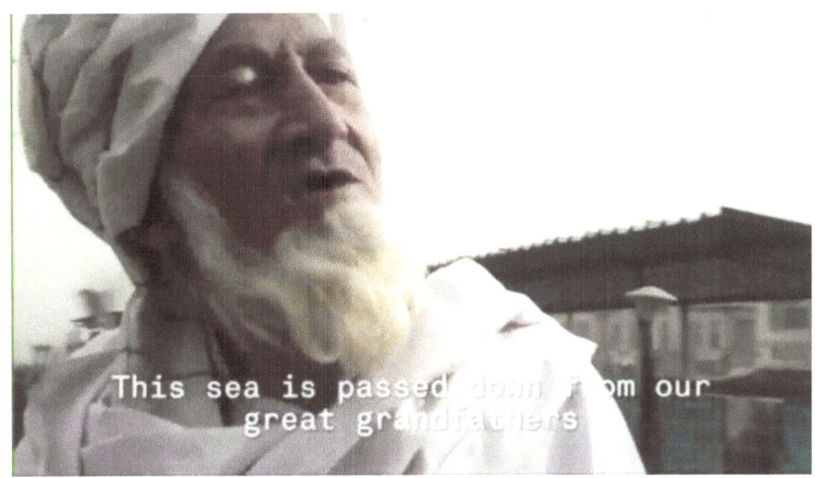

Alka Sadat, still from *The Kabul Sea*, undated.

Alka Sadat's *The Kabul Sea* documents the curious belief of many in arid, landlocked Afghanistan that the Kabul River is in fact a sea. It dries in certain seasons and in others the "sea" is a place of ritual and celebration.

Every Drop a World

In 2007, activist/writer/curator Lucy R. Lippard, through the inspired agency of EcoArts Connections (formerly EcoArts) founder-director Marda Kirn and the Boulder (Colorado) Museum of Contemporary Art[7] produced a blockbuster exhibition, *Weather Report: Art and Climate Change*. In 2013, as flooding decimated much of the area and many of the communities around Boulder, photographer Subhankar Banerjee, who had participated in *Weather Report*, reminded readers in a *ClimateStoryTellers* essay[8] of the exhibit's prescience in predicting an event few imagined could be so intense. A month after the disaster, Gluckstern visited the town of Lyons, one of the worst-hit communities, and shot *lyons, co, 10-10-13*, a silent, tender tour of the devastation.

Patrizia Monzani's *found footage* briefly narrates the history of humanity starting with our amoebic origins and moving into our increasingly oblivious, desacralized relationship to the planet, using archival material from the Internet movie database, opensource films. In Robin Johnston's hypnagogic *Death of Light in Symmetry*, light and water gradually unite into another vision of time's progress.

Liz Marshall's *Excerpt from Water on the Table* is just that: an outtake from her award-winning feature film. This portion focuses on a First Nations community living downstream from Alberta, Canada's tar sands at Fort Chipewyan, where the water is poisoned and there are high rates of cancer. The film follows Canadian activist Maude Barlow, who crusades tirelessly to have water declared a human right and protected from privatization.[9]

Pyaasi (The Thirsty), a musical film by the Indian folk-rock group Swarathma, is inspired by the politicization of the South Indian River Cauvery, which for 200 years has been in violent dispute over distribution of waters. In impoverished areas around the world, women and girls spend hours a day collecting water for domestic use. "This," environmental scholar James Salzman writes, "squeezes out their opportunities for employment or education, perpetuating gender inequality and poverty … [P]roviding drinking water to poor communities can transform lives … [but] the search for private capital to provide local water has unleashed furious globalization battles where proponents of privatization clash against claims for a human right to water."[10]

Evan Abramson and Carmen Elsa Lopez note that 99 percent of people in Western Province, Kenya, lack access to clean water. Their award-winning film, *Carbon for Water*, describes the ironies of how, in order to make the water safe, the people must boil it with wood. Deforestation is rampant in the once-lush land and waterborne diseases kill thousands there each year. Indeed, worldwide, unsafe drinking water is the single leading source of mortality in the developing world, particularly among children.

Jessica Plumb's *Climate Change: An Intimate Portrait* witnesses glaciers melting in Alaska. Plumb describes the sound of dripping water as her most enduring memory during the filming of this tragic reminder of global warming, as glaciers recede and oceans rise.

Meanwhile, the water in Beth Block's *Leaky Mountain* is ferocious. Thousands of gallons of water rush violently from a broken pipe, unnoticed, creating a vast waterfall plunging into a desiccated canyon still suffering from a two-year drought. And in Pat Law's *Voyage*, an eerie, automated voice repeats a spooky weather report – "dry," "dry," "dry" – over the shadow of a ship's bow wriggling like a monster through the water.

Light of the Storm, by Georgie Friedman, was filmed at night during the intensity and unpredictability of a lightning storm, forcing us to remember how completely vulnerable we are to Nature's perilous power.

Finally, calm anger in Samizay's *This Will be the Last*, as a woman washes sheets in a tub. Then, once again, Houston provides us with a tantalizing postscript in *Indonesian Borneo: Rain Meditation*, a final paean, a healing song.[11]

This catalogue is centered on still images from the exhibition's films and videos accompanied by material from the show's wall texts, which list facts about water – consumption, drought, flooding, pollution, and other ongoing calamities – along with quotations and a few poems. The facts listed here do not provide a complete picture of our water crisis, but will, I hope, give an idea of what we are up against and perhaps some clues about how we might help avert disaster.

Gratitude to the munificent funders and folk involved in producing *Water, Water Everywhere* can be found in the front of this catalogue. Their support and partnership are immeasurable. In addition, I thank Ismail Serageldin, founding director of Egypt's Bibliotheca Alexandrina and founder and former chairman of the Global Water Partnership, for his generous foreword, Betsy Damon, founder/director of Keepers of the Waters, for her excellent and passionate essay, Karen Leggett Abouraya for her ongoing encouragement and support, and Andrew Wille for his invaluable editing advice. Profound appreciation, as well, to poets E.J. McAdams, Elizabeth Robinson, Mark DuCharme, Michael Wolfe, and Jack Collom for their wonderful contributions. Thanks also to Mary Sweet and Soma Honkanen of Sweet Design, to Kate P. Heath for her beautiful drawings for "Questions About Water," and to *Water, Water Everywhere*'s many hosts – galleries, museums, and community groups – past, present, and future. They are visionaries who understand the terrible urgency we face.

---

[1] Jack Collom, *Second Nature* (Berkeley, CA: Instance Press, 2012).

[2] Steven Mithen, *Thirst: Water and Power in the Ancient World* (Cambridge, MA: Harvard University Press, 2012), 3.

[3] Mithen, *Thirst*, 5.

[4] Lewis Carroll, *Through the Looking Glass*, (New York: Grosset & Dunlap, Inc., 1946), 201.

[5] James Salzman, *Drinking Water: A History*, (New York: Overlook Duckworth, Peter Mayer Publishers, Inc., 2012), 21.

[6] James Salzman, *Drinking Water*, 119-122.

[7] BMoCA co-directors Joan Markowitz and Penny Barnow and associate curator Kristen Gerdes must be credited, too, for their amazing work on *Weather Report*, a truly historic endeavor.

[8] Subhankar Banerjee, ClimateStorytellers, "Boulder Flooding: Remembering Warnings from *Weather Report*," September 13, 2013, www.climatestorytellers.org/stories/subhankar-banerjee-boulder-flooding.

[9] Maude Barlow is the National Chairperson of the Council of Canadians, a citizens' advocacy organization with members and chapters across Canada. Many of her talks have been documented by Alternative Radio and can be accessed at www.alternativeradio.org. Also available on Alternative Radio are interviews with Canadian journalist Andrew Nikiforuk, author of *Tar Sands: Dirty Oil and the Future of a Continent* (Vancouver, Canada: Greystone Books, 2010), a critical exposé of the world's largest energy project—the Alberta oil sands—that has made Canada one of the worst environmental offenders on Earth.

[10] James Salzman, *Drinking Water*, 21.

[11] Paean – from the ancient Greek, "a song of joy, praise, or victory," originally, "a healing song."

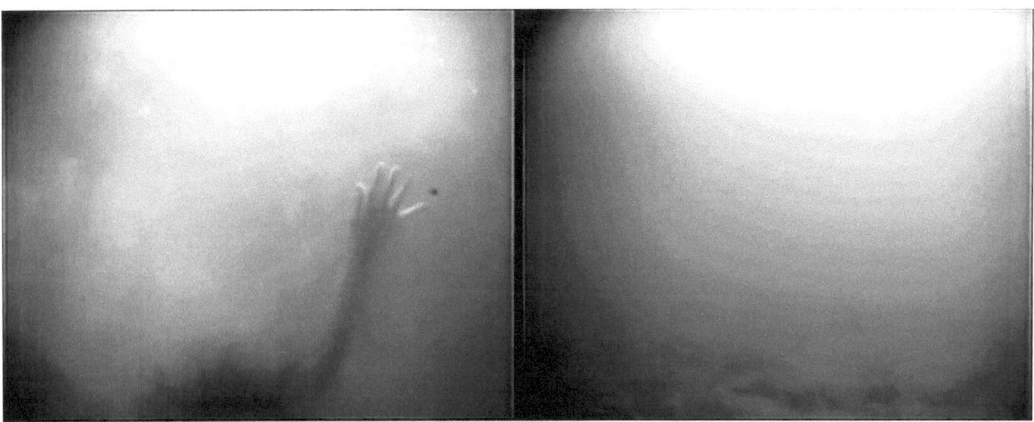

Mary Rachel Fanning, still from *The Trophy*, 2009.

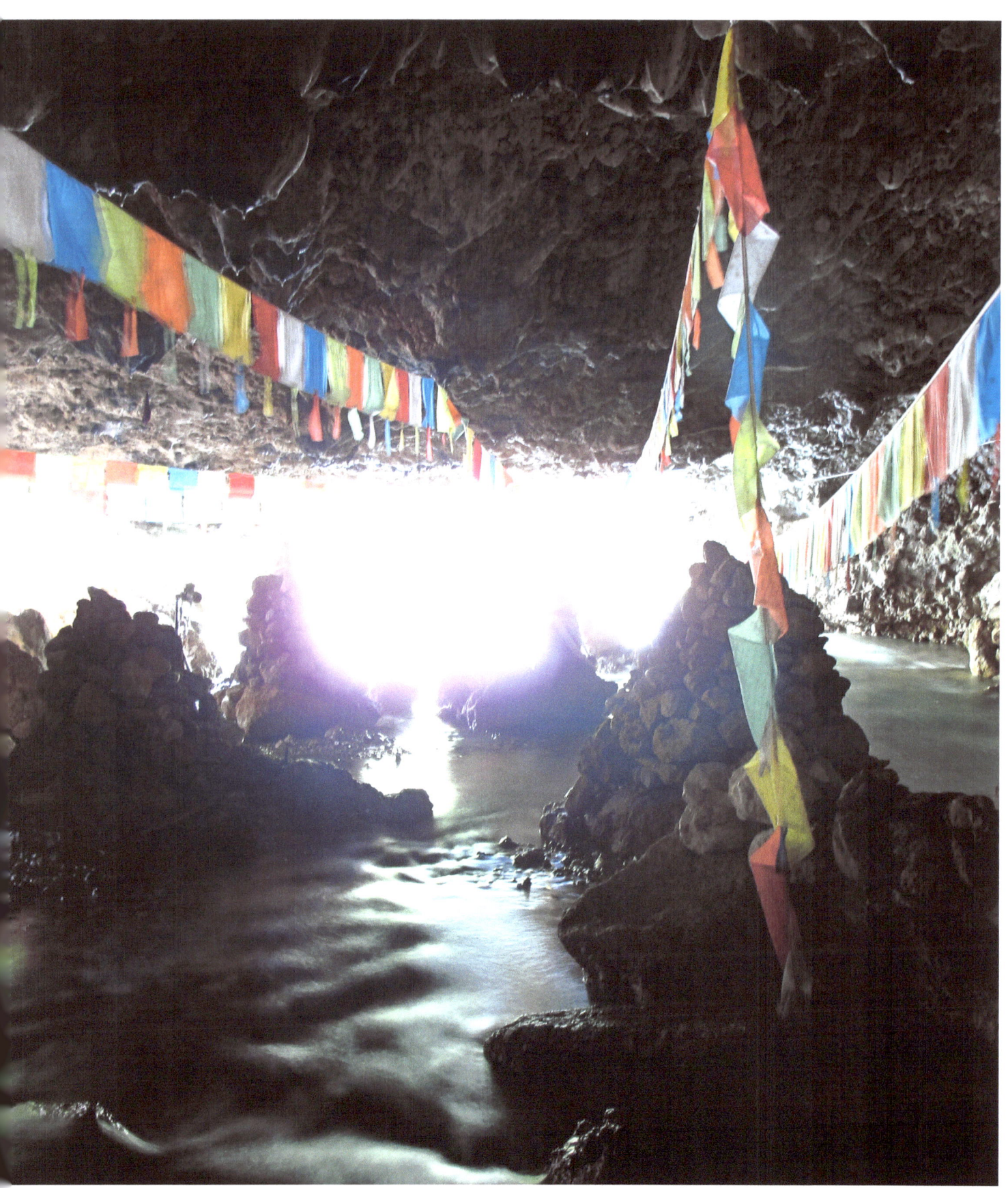
From the project *Resources: Saving Living Systems*. Water rushes out of the Badalama Cave in Muli County, Sichuan China. Courtesy Betsy Damon, Keepers of the Waters.

Remembering the Source

Betsy Damon

I have come to understand water as a profoundly aggressive element, one that makes life on this Earth possible. The water molecule is the most flexible that we know. It organizes and reorganizes itself depending on the situation. We experience it as a solid, a liquid, and gas, but it also can become a dense gel that is found in our cells. Water holds shape and performs thousands of functions in our bodies, many of which we do not yet understand. How has it happened that this miraculous substance has been reduced to a commodity, a simplicity with a price tag?

For thousands of years humans have interacted with the planet's water, sometimes with reverence, often with destruction. Today, there are nearly seven billion people on the planet. It is a time of unprecedented invention and materialism, and it appears these forces have drawn a straight line toward ecological destruction.

There is too little regard for the complex role of water in creating life and sustaining ecosystems. We have straightened rivers, drained lakes and wetlands, and pumped aquifers dry. We use the waters as our sewers. Every chemical we use on our lawns, farms, and homes – from fire retardants to antibiotics to pesticides – ends up in our waters. Upland water sources, the final frontier, are rapidly being destroyed by climate change and development. If the sources of our rivers are eradicated and compromised, what will flow downstream to nurture the thousands of miles of living systems below?

Our civilization has forgotten how complex our relationship is to water, and we are forgetting more and more. Ivan Illich, in his prophetic book, *H2O and the Waters of Forgetfulness*, believes that with the ease of piped water in our homes, we are forgetting water's natural sources. We cannot take care of what we have forgotten, what no longer exists in our minds. We cannot take care of rivers if we never see a river running because it has been buried or polluted. If you believe that water magically comes from a pipe, and never question its origins and where it goes after it leaves your home, you have forgotten. If you forget that your body is water, and that you were born in water, and that every human depends on water, just like you, then it is easy to throw chemicals into the waters.

The exhibition, *Water, Water Everywhere: Paean to a Vanishing Resource*, poses the question: how can art impact the way we think about water and its vast issues? Let us start with the artist. In the midst of a corporate culture of conformity, isolation, and oppression, there are people who make different choices – many of these are artists. The artist is often free from certain constraints, who likes to invent, challenge, start something, who dares to follow his or her heart and mind.

Artists are multifaceted. With many skills and abilities, artists create conversation, tangible works, and action. They innovate. They build relationships and alternative communities. They find different ways to inform, envision, and provide practical solutions. We can perhaps consider all the artists out there as an army. We are not organized as such – we are an invisible army, one that does not stop, that does not give up. We are turning people's attention to water, to the environment, and living systems. We are creating the images, language, and actions for those whose voices are unheard and suppressed, and whose images are censored.

Technology has transformed our world and too often we have ignored the complexity and fundamental imperative of water as the foundation of all. Technology is not going to save our water sources – culture will. I have worked in the Eastern Himalayas, where I encountered the Tibetan culture, which honors its water. Their sacred water sites have origin stories, cautionary tales, and narratives for use. Their water is seen as medicine and connected to their health and the health of the environment. Globalization and development are bringing many changes to the Tibetans. Their culture is being destroyed, and so are the waters.

We need ways to know and remember where our water comes from. We need to remember that we are a community held together by water. We need to know what clean, healthy water looks like, and that it is complex and has intricate form. Culture is where artists play their hand, where our invisible army rallies. We are creating culture and exposing truths. When greed and materialism dominate, artists can provide hope where it might not otherwise be found. Thankfully, in our time, we are seeing artists, scientists, community activists, engineers, and, yes, governing bodies, collaborating to face and address the pressing issues of water.

Water is a human right. Water is an Earth right. Water is the right to life.

Forty years ago, Betsy Damon stepped outside her traditional art training and carved a unique path to work with the environment, communities, science, and art. Her public engagement began with gritty art performances on the New York City streets. In the 1970s, she engaged in the women's movement, and in

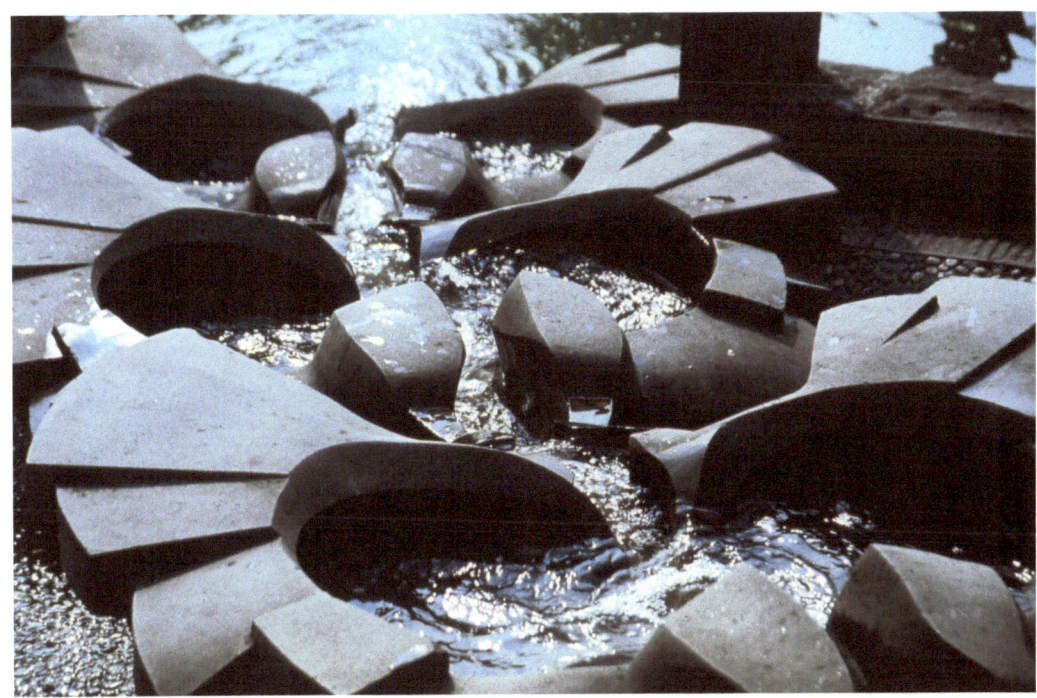

Flow-form structures in *The Living Water Garden* in Chengdu, China, at the headwaters to a major tributary of the Yangzi River. Courtesy Betsy Damon, Keepers of the Waters.

1982 founded the support network, No Limits for Women Artists.

In 1985, after a cross-country camping trip with her children, Damon found herself reconnected to the primal elements of the natural world – the sound of wind, the flow of water, the forest, the rain. This initiated the casting of a 250-foot dry riverbed, The Memory of Clean Water, *which brought her attention to the invisible destruction that development was having on water sources. In the early evening, while casting the riverbed, Damon looked up to realize that the stones of the riverbed were patterned like the stars of the sky, that everywhere there are the patterns of water.*

In 1991, Damon founded Keepers of the Waters, through which she creates grassroots and community-based models of water stewardship, including sculpture, teaching, lectures, and workshops. In China, she created the nation's first public art event for the environment, and the Living Water Garden, *a world renowned public park and natural water filtration model.*

Today Betsy Damon continues her work, with projects such as ReSources: Saving Living Systems, *documenting the living Tibetan water culture in the Eastern Himalayas, and* Living Waters of Larimer: A Fresh Infrastructure, *a project for community action and sustainable water infrastructure in Pittsburgh, Pennsylvania.*

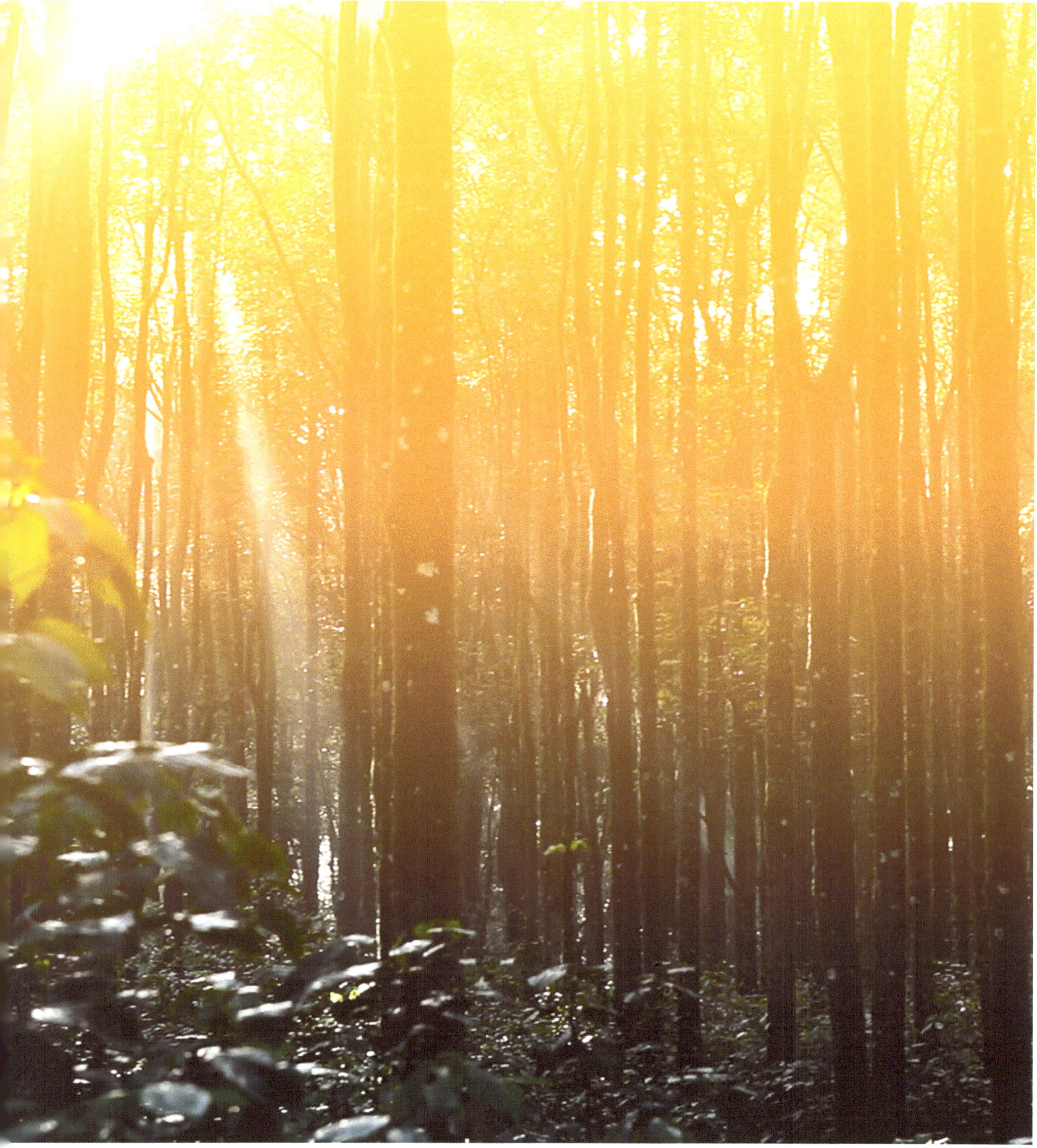

Evan Abramson & Carmen Elsa Lopez, still from *Carbon for Water*, 2011.

Currents and Divides

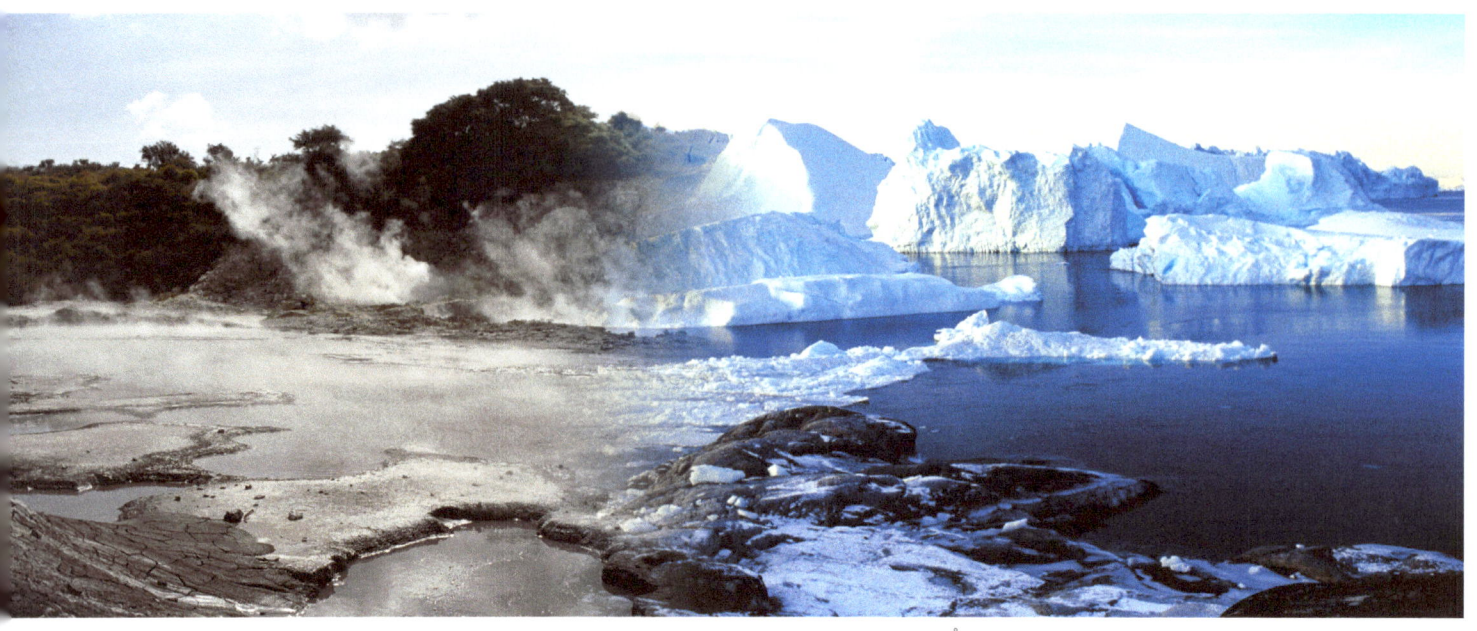

Åsa Maria Bengtsson and Ewa Cederstam, still from *FLOW*, 2006.

An average U.S. family of four uses up to 260 gallons of water in the home per day.

A typical individual in the United States uses 500 liters of water each day. The recommended daily water requirement for sanitation, bathing, cooking, and consumption is approximately 50 liters per person per day. Over 1 billion people use less than 6 liters per day.

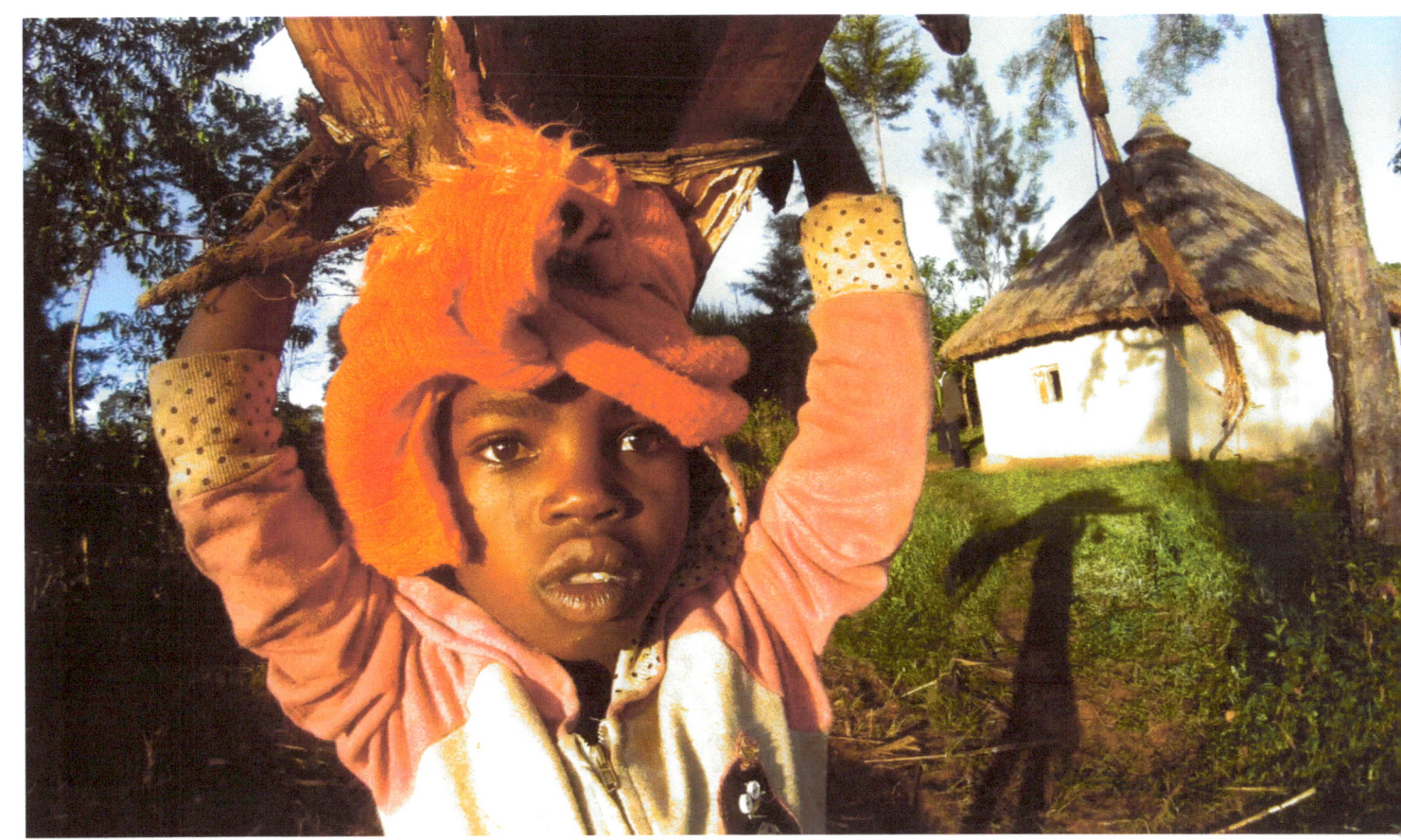

Evan Abramson and Carmen Elsa Lopez, still from *Carbon for Water*, 2011.

"The only path to a water-secure future is water conservation, source water protection, watershed restoration, and the just and equitable sharing of the water resources of the planet. Water is a commons, a public trust, and a human right and no one has the right to appropriate it for profit when others are dying from lack of access."

– Maude Barlow, National Chairperson of The Council of Canadians, co-founder of the Blue Planet Project

To still be held, against an atrocity. Some of this is vague. Things go on without repeating. *One atrocity leads to another, I know.* Some of this is whispered. In childhood, it was simpler— this folly, the seemingly ambient skies. At the edges of some moment we aren't sure. This is a lyrical fable.

This is a fable, but not lyrical. It's been reported from the front that you don't breathe. One of our poets is here to investigate, though his grasp of the material is not certain. The material is uncertain. It's formed by skies which are fleeting. It is formed by oceans, gulls or pieces of brick affixed to great white sheets of paper. Nightfall is a coincidence of sleep— a tenuous redaction to the unspoken notions already at stake. The moon does not trust us [yet]. The sun is yellow. The atrocities are hidden behind a curtain ~~camera~~. To hear them whimpering ~~to form a public language~~ we have to keep them there.

This is a private language. Death is speaking. There is oil to burn. This is silent, so it forms a rupture. Its alternative is silence, but not rapture. On the condition of speaking publicly without saying anything. The alternative will not ~~yet~~ drown ~~us~~. It is a public sentencing. Burning, as in silence. *To dream where shadows forge the edges of the rain.* Burning, as in life [faces you don't come back to]. No one sees all the dead faces, the dead gulls who don't cry. Yet we lie awake in silence. Waiting for history to erupt.

– Mark DuCharme
From *The Unfinished: Books I-VI*
Originally appeared in Poets for Living Waters

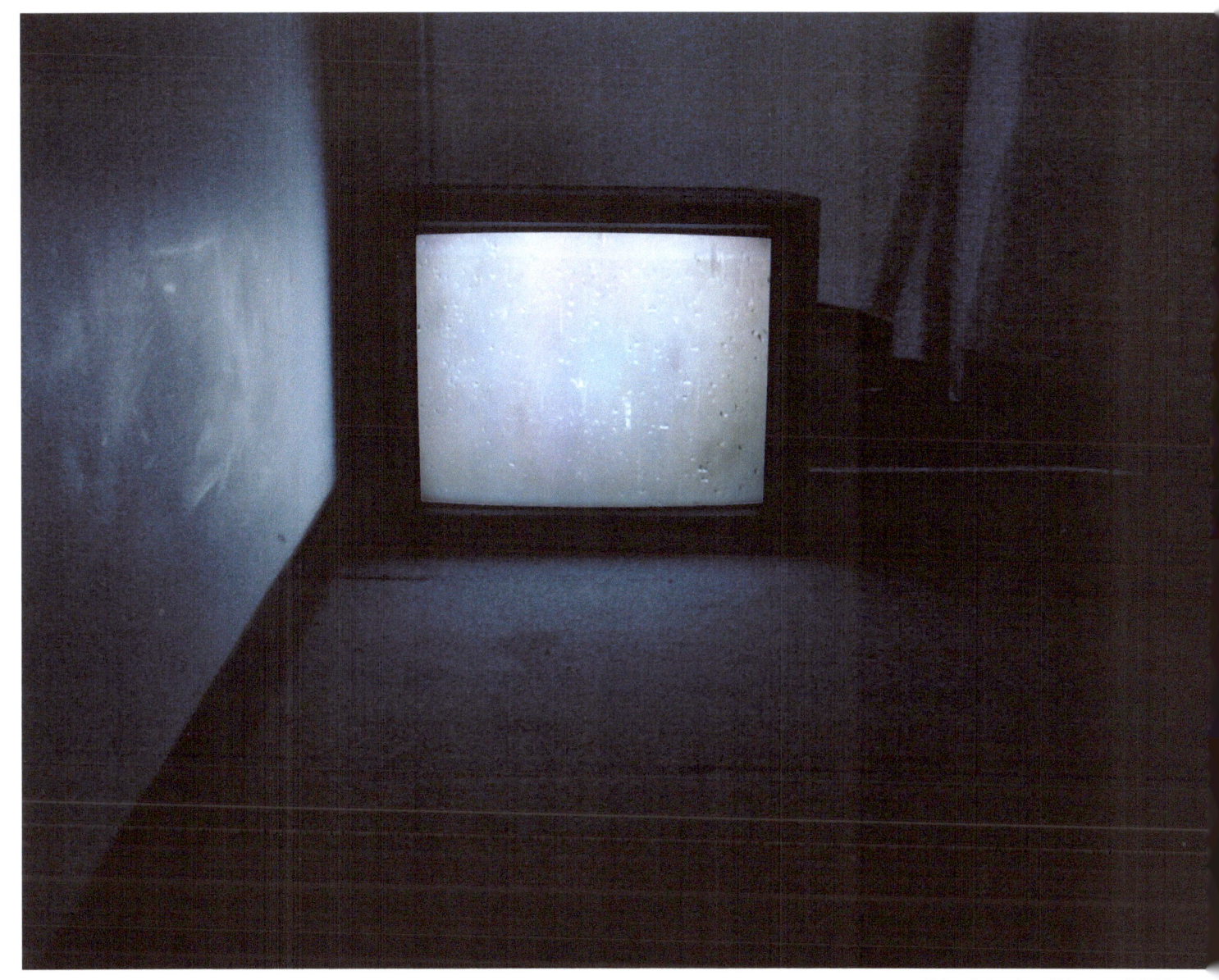

Ruben Aubrecht, still from *april*, 2005.

Agriculture is responsible for about 70% of the world's water usage. Industry uses a further 22%.

Americans are only 5% of the world's population, but they consume 26% of the world's energy, about 15 times more per person in developing countries.

More than 1.5 billion people do not have access to clean, safe water.

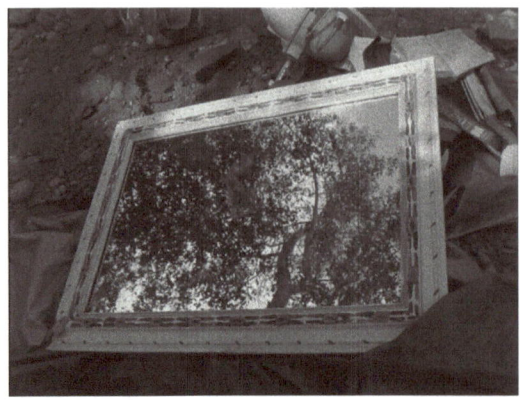

J. Gluckstern, still from *lyons, co, 10-10-13*, 2013.

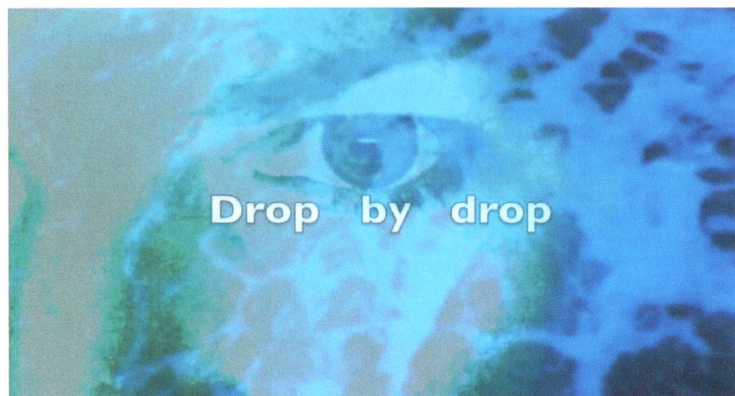

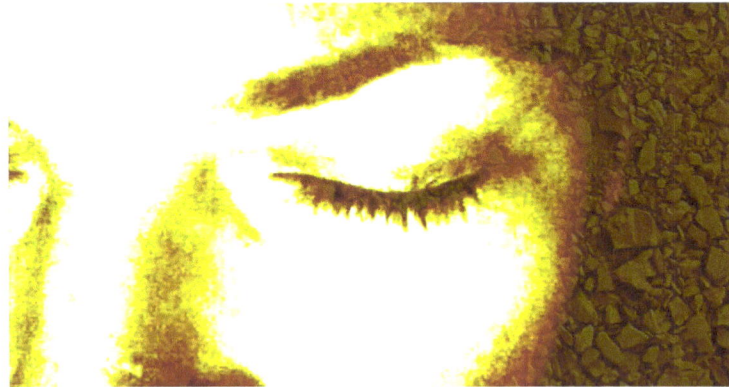

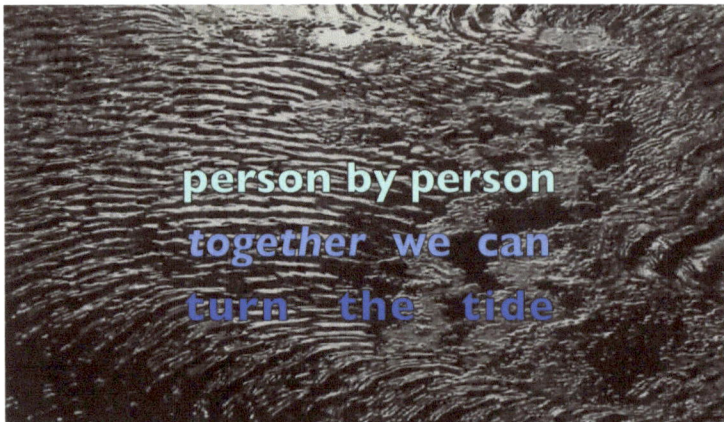

Krisanne Baker, stills from *World Water Crisis*.

A full bath is equal to approximately 60 gallons of water.

An American taking a 5-minute shower uses more water than the average person in a developing country slum uses for an entire day.

No country uses water more sparingly than Singapore, which employs education, water rationing, recycled wastewater, rainwater collection, and an excellent government water management program. Per capita water use fell from 44 gallons a day in 2003 to 41 gallons per day in 2011.

On Water (from Elizabeth to Jenny)

It touches its own body to measure ambiguity.

    Where do I go, asks the hand of the touch:

    gas, liquid, solid.

    I am not who I am.

What was once blue, was green, white, black, translucent.

    And is so again.

Water mates with itself, a lover falling hard through

soft, betraying through trustworthy, torrent through

opacity.

    All that we knew of each other in our form,

    where do I go, blunt and insinuating.

    The touch paired with itself. A humid air.

The point of contact as it bathes and thirsts.

A hand on a real body, its mutable fact.

– Elizabeth Robinson

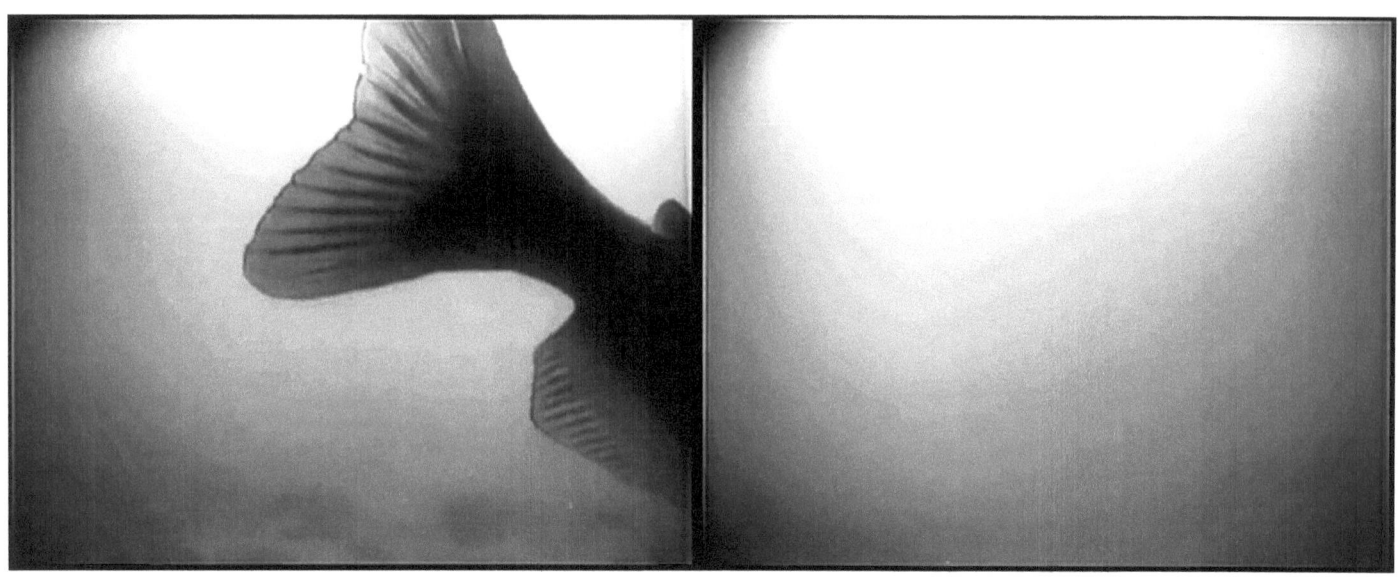

Mary Rachel Fanning, still from *The Trophy*, 2009.

Running tap water for 2 minutes is equal to 3-5 gallons of water.

On average, women in Africa and Asia walk 3.7 miles daily to collect water.

A 5-minute shower is equal to 20-35 gallons of water.

The average dishwasher uses over 100 liters of water per cycle.

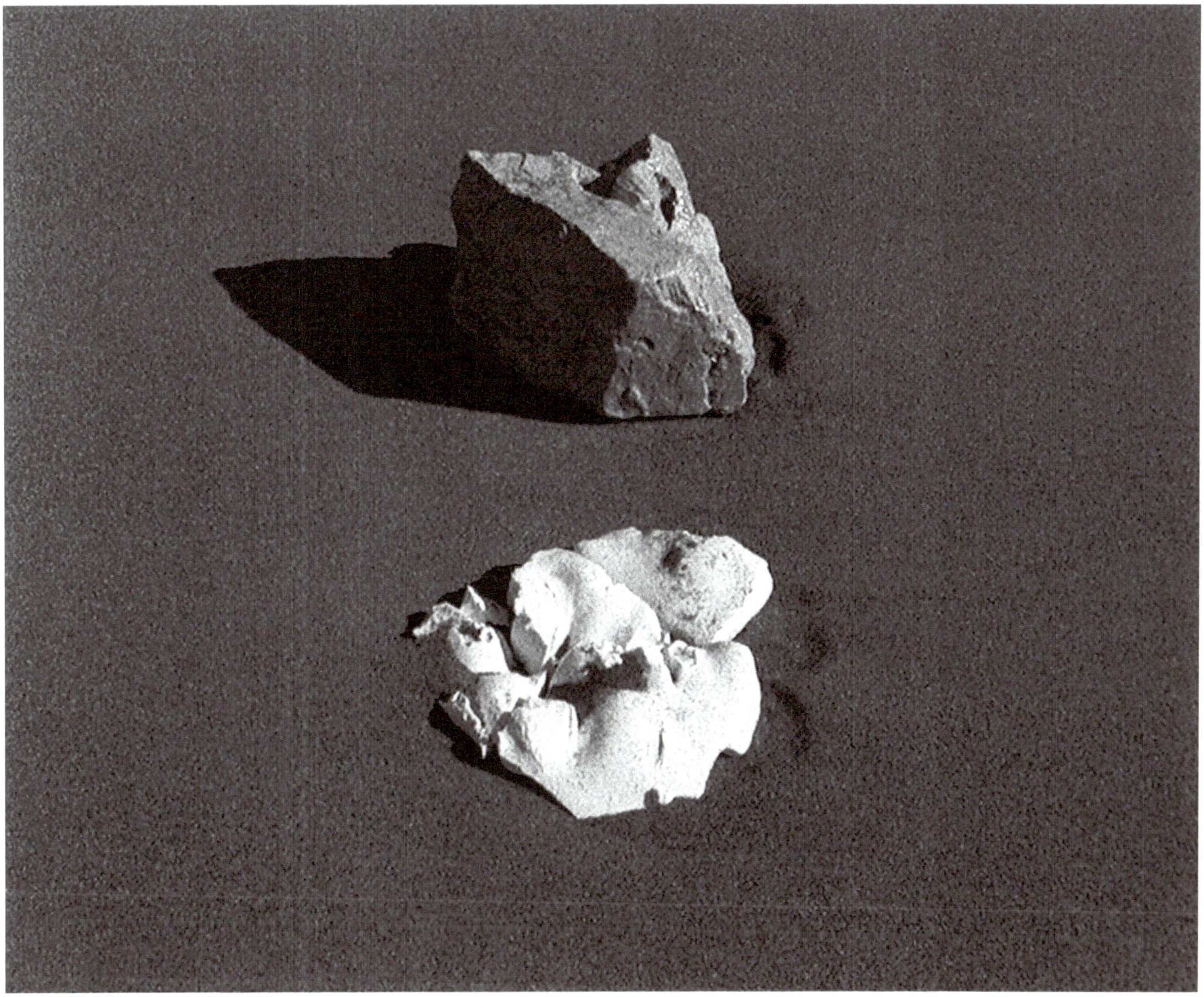

Diego Fiori, still from *Silenzio*, undated

The average toilet uses 8 liters of clean water in a single flush.

Water consumption in an average U.S. household is 8 times that of an Indian household.

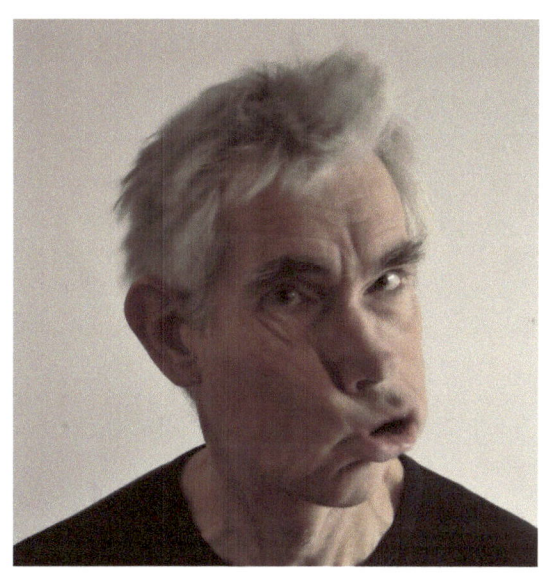

Jaap Blonk, still from *Flababble 1*, 2011.

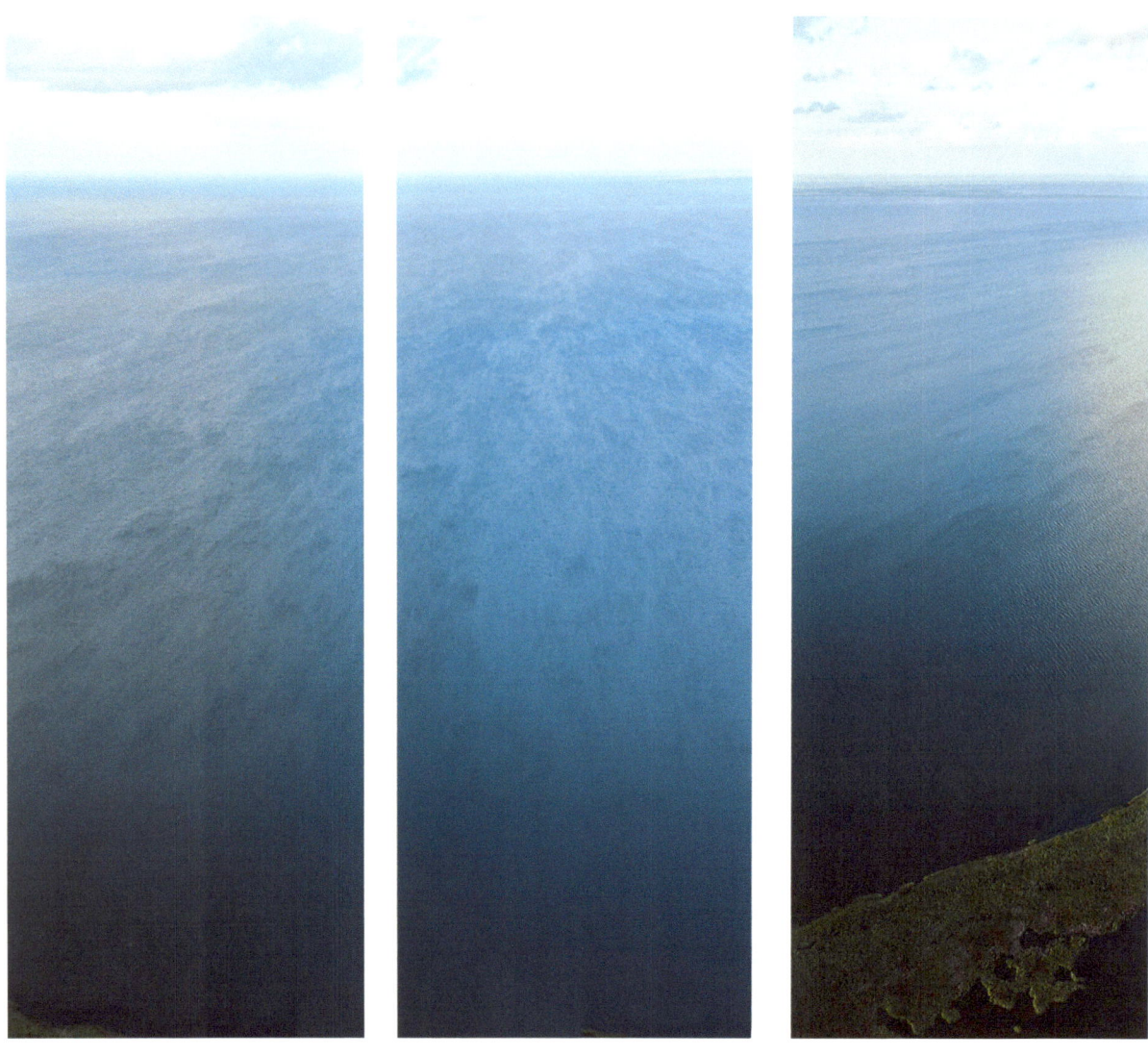

"God has cared for these trees, saved them from drought, disease, avalanches, and a thousand tempests and floods. But he cannot save them from fools."

– John Muir, Scottish-born American naturalist, author, early advocate of wilderness preservation in the United States

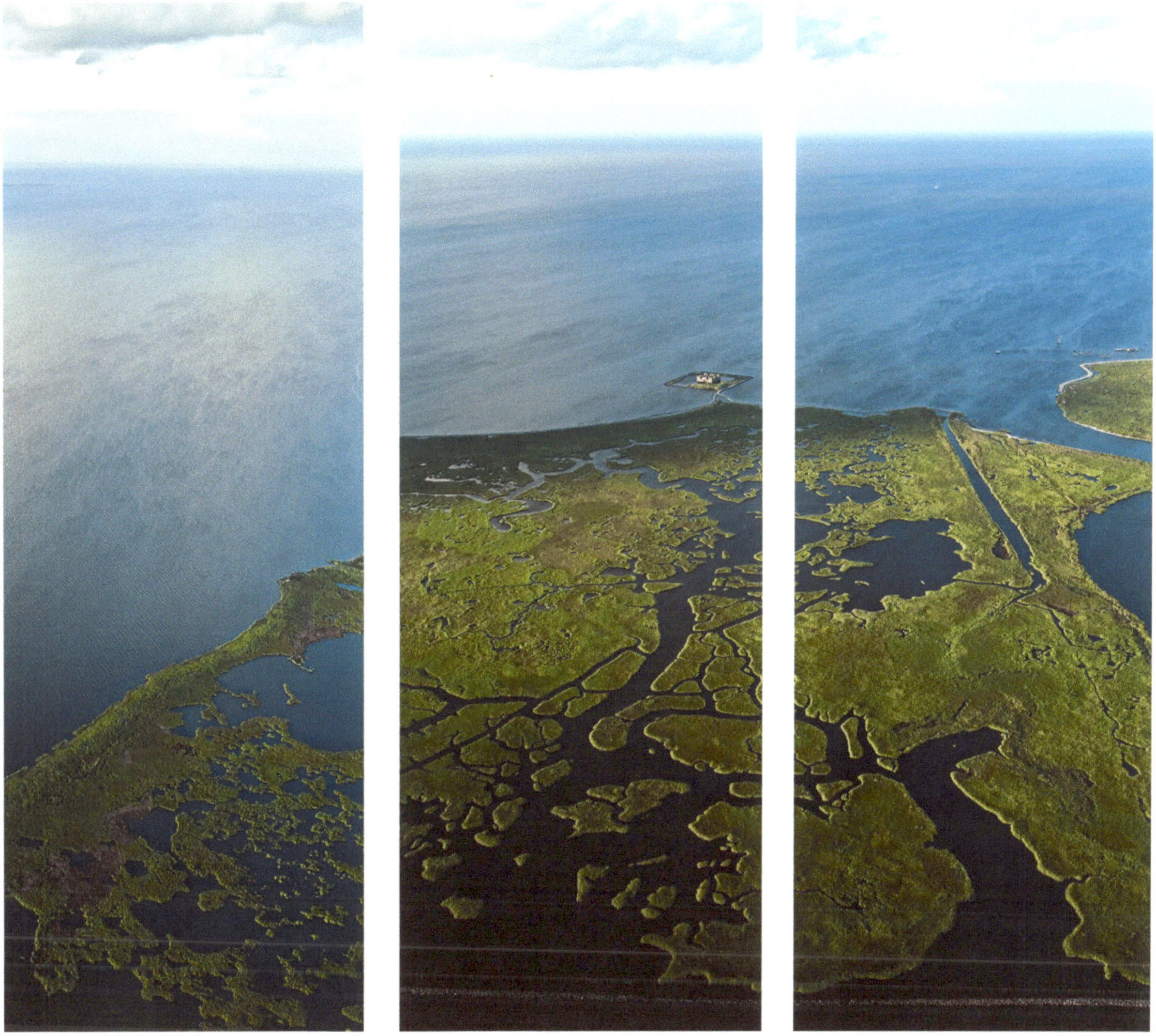

Michel Varisco, still from *Shifting*, 2012.

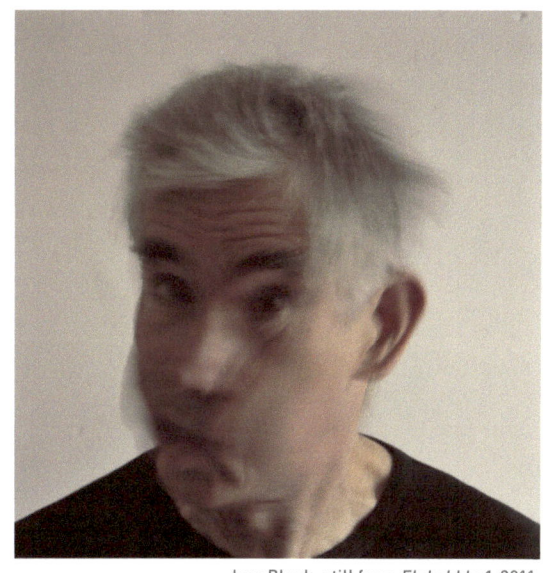

Jaap Blonk, still from *Flababble 1*, 2011.

"If the wars of this century were fought over oil, the wars of the next century will be fought over water – unless we change our approach to managing this precious and vital resource."

– Ismail Serageldin, founding director of the Bibliotheca Alexandrina (Egypt) and founder and former chairman of the Global Water Partnership.

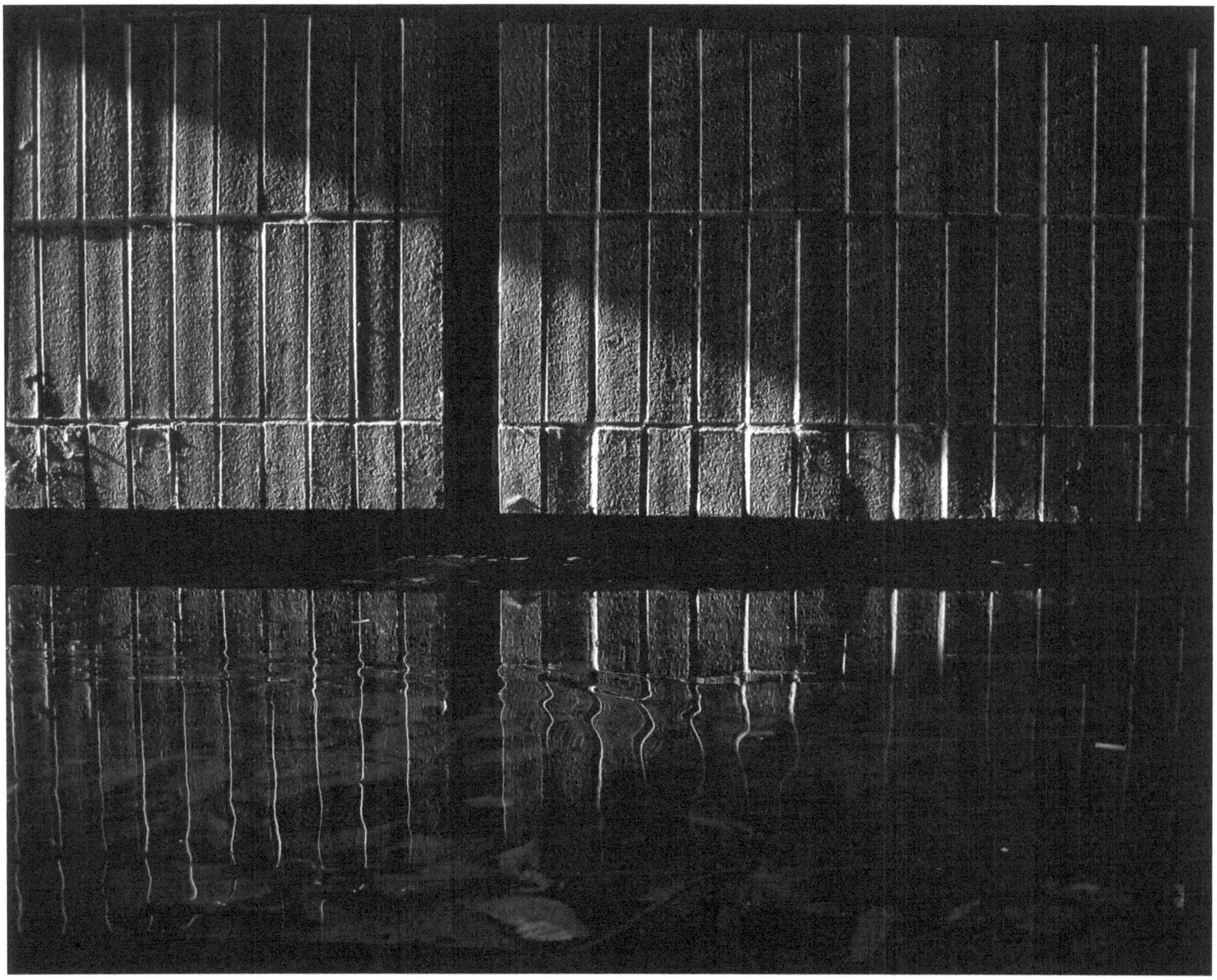

Robin Johnston, still from *Death of Light in Symmetry*, 2011.

Since the 1970s, the percentage of Earth's land area stricken by serious drought has more than doubled. Global warming is largely blamed.

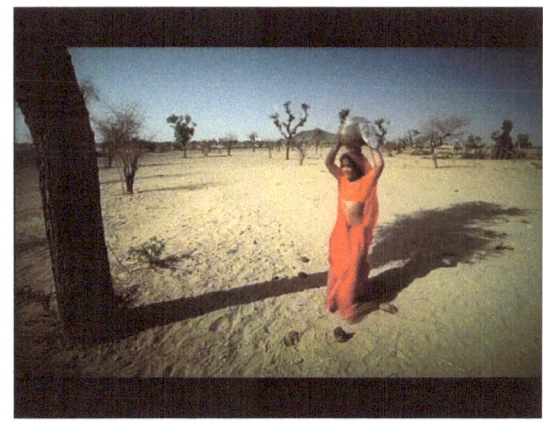

Swarathma, still from *Pyassi (The Thirsty)*, undated.

In developing countries, drought may affect people's access to food, as well as water.

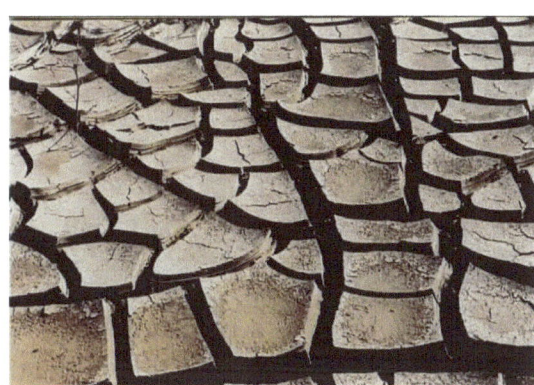

Basia Irland, still from *Book of Drought: A Water Memory*, 2009.

Droughts are a common feature of climate in California, Colorado, Georgia, and New York, as well as in Brazil, Southeast Asia, Southern Africa, and Australia.

Some of the world's largest cities – Melbourne, Australia; Barcelona, Spain; and Mexico City – have already experienced drought emergencies.

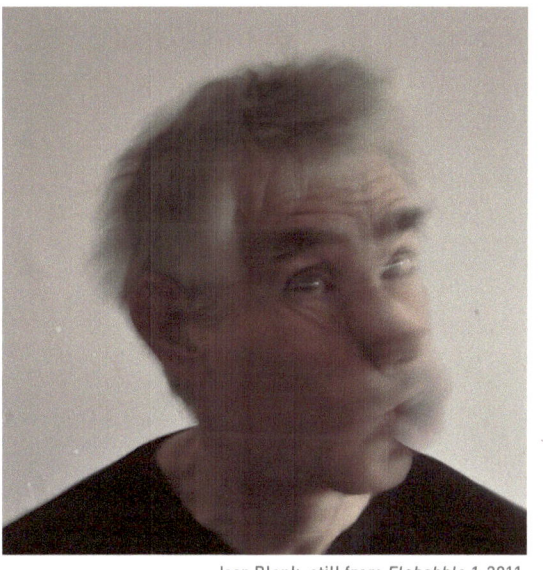

Jaap Blonk, still from *Flababble 1*, 2011.

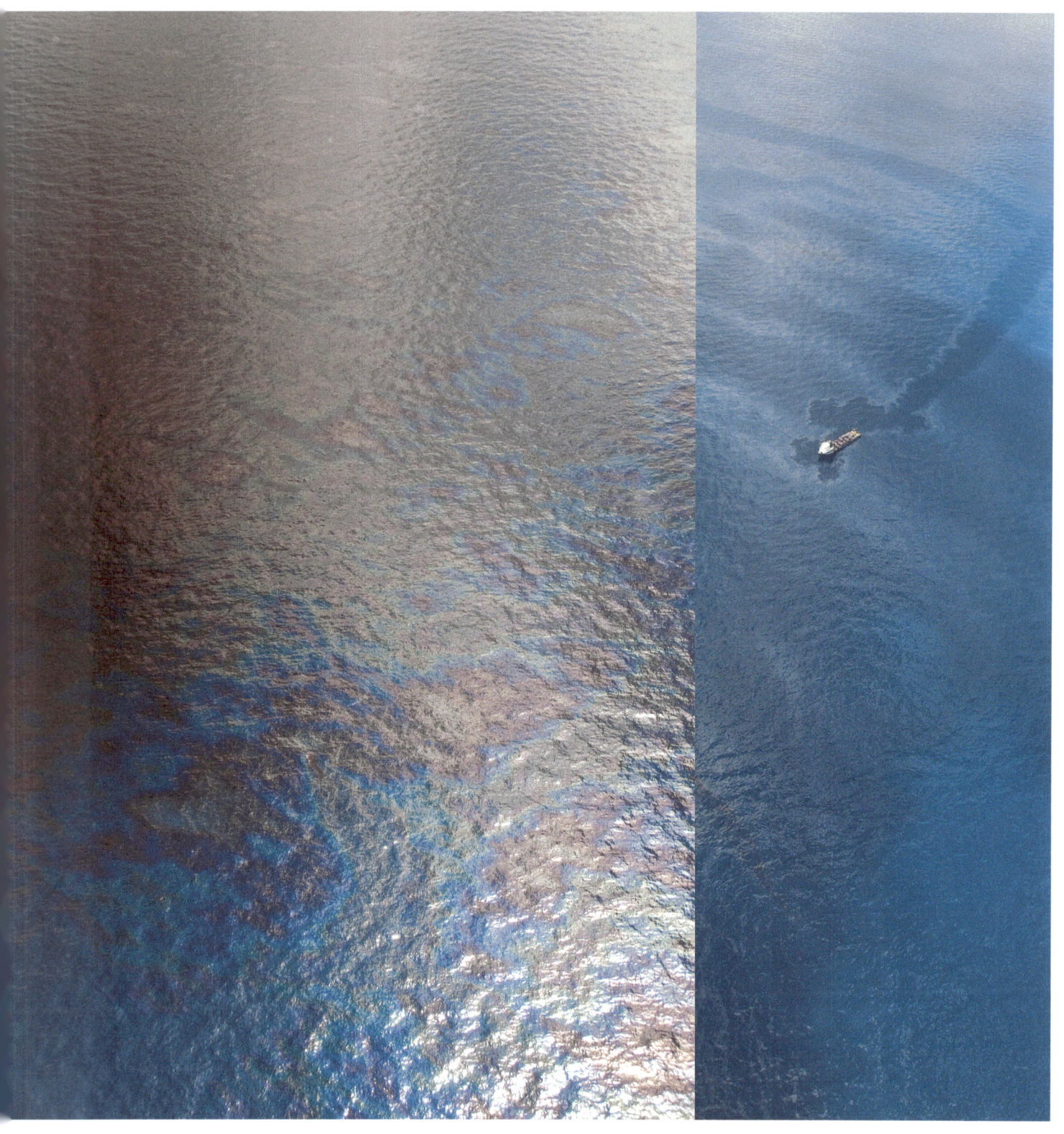

"Earth provides enough to satisfy every man's needs, but not every man's greed."

– Mahatma Gandhi

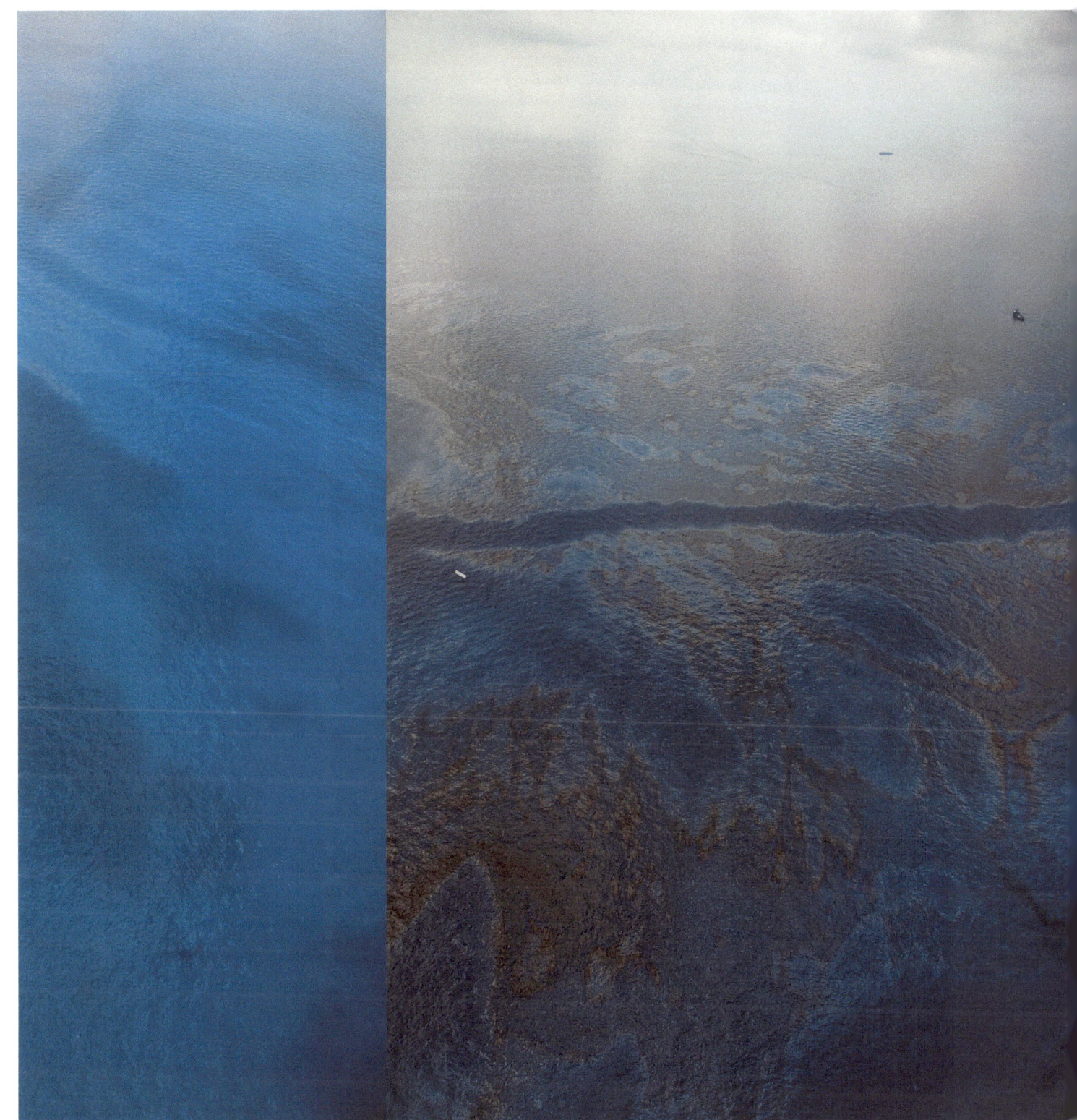

Michel Varisco, still from *Shifting*, 2012.

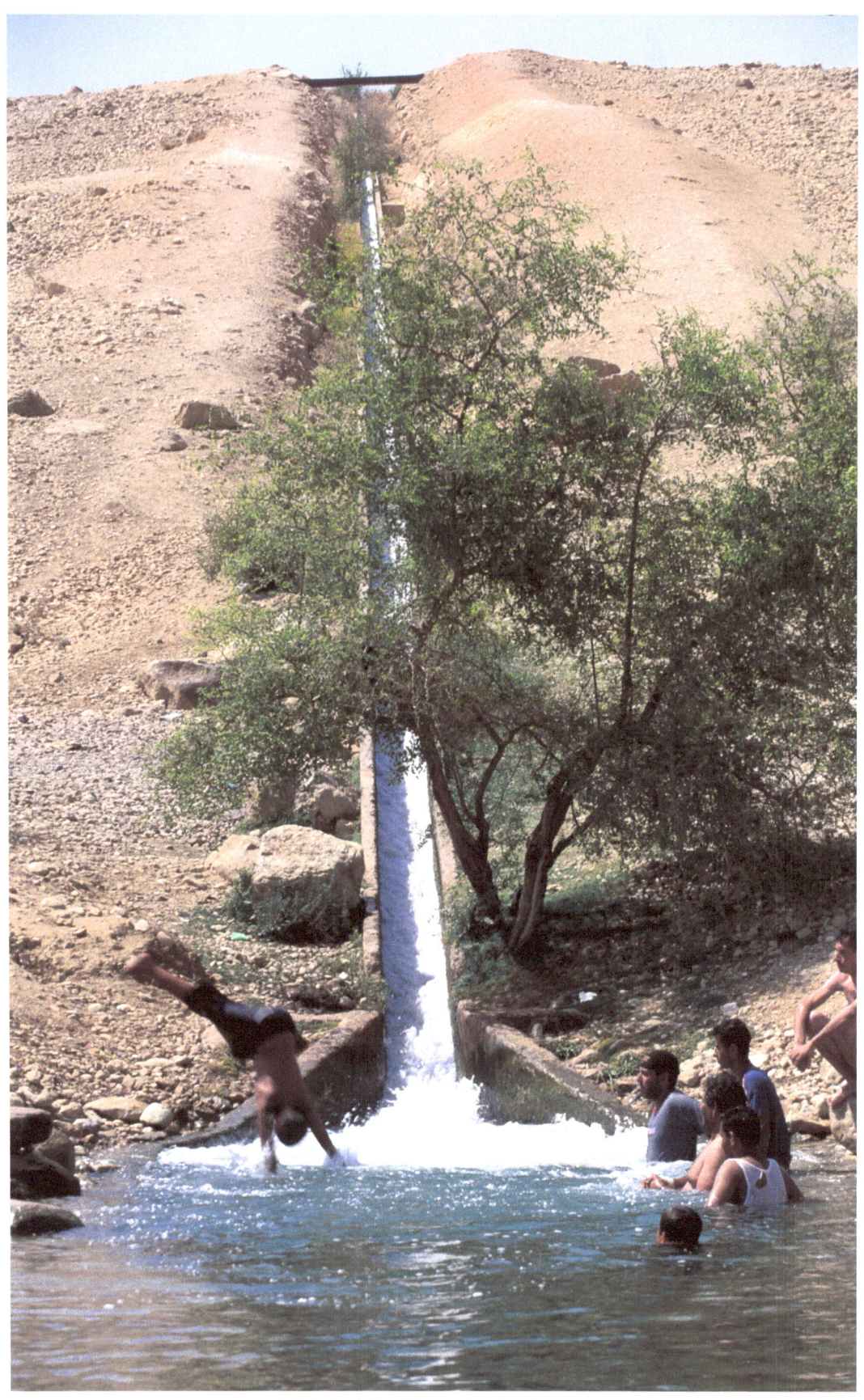

Auja Spring, before. Friends of the Earth Middle East still from *Good Water Neighbors*, 2011.

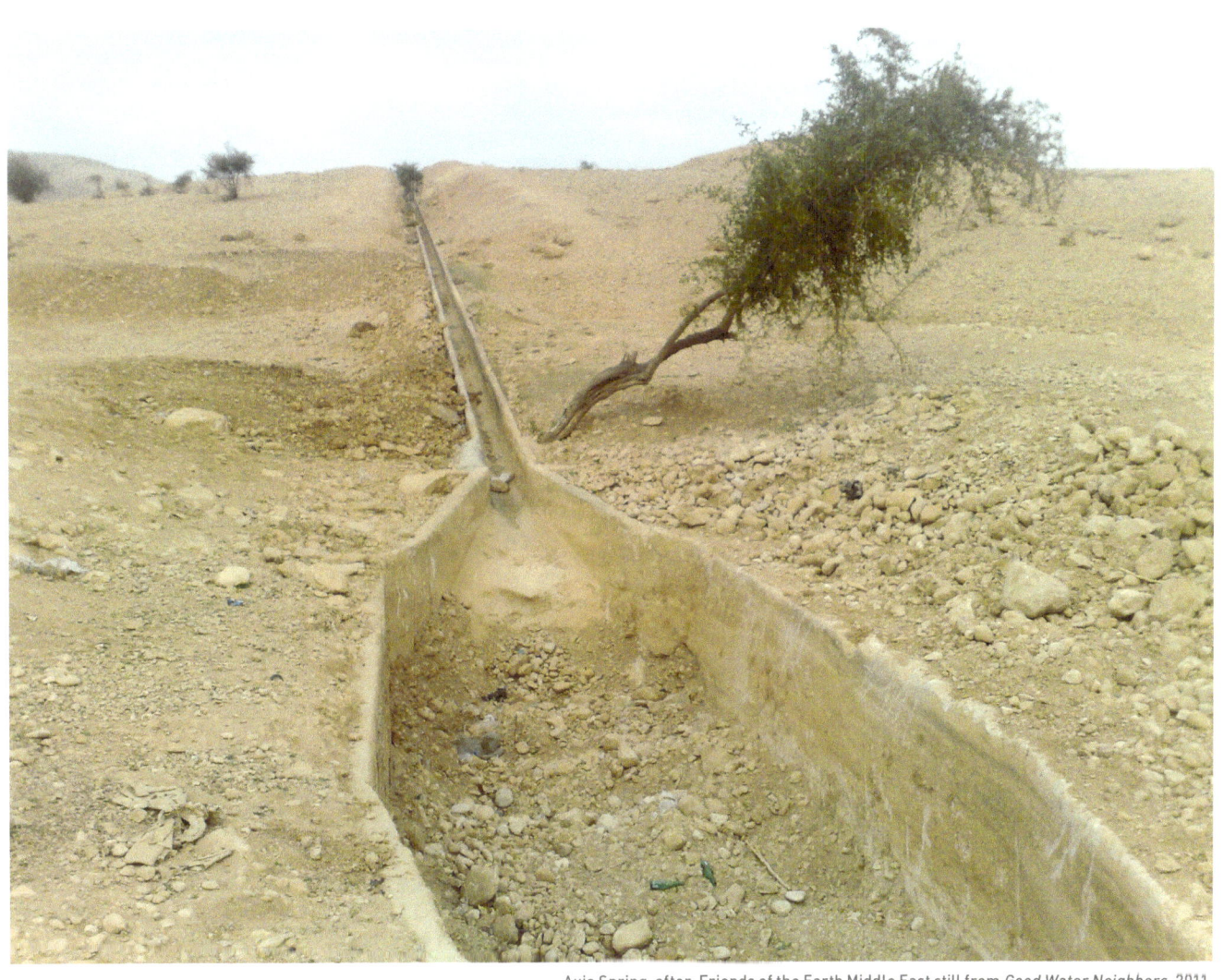

Auja Spring, after. Friends of the Earth Middle East still from *Good Water Neighbors*, 2011.

As the climate heats up, droughts are expected to become more frequent and severe in some locations.

In Sub-Saharan Africa, women spend on average 16 hours per week collecting water.

Climatologists call drought a "creeping disaster," because its effects are not all felt at once.

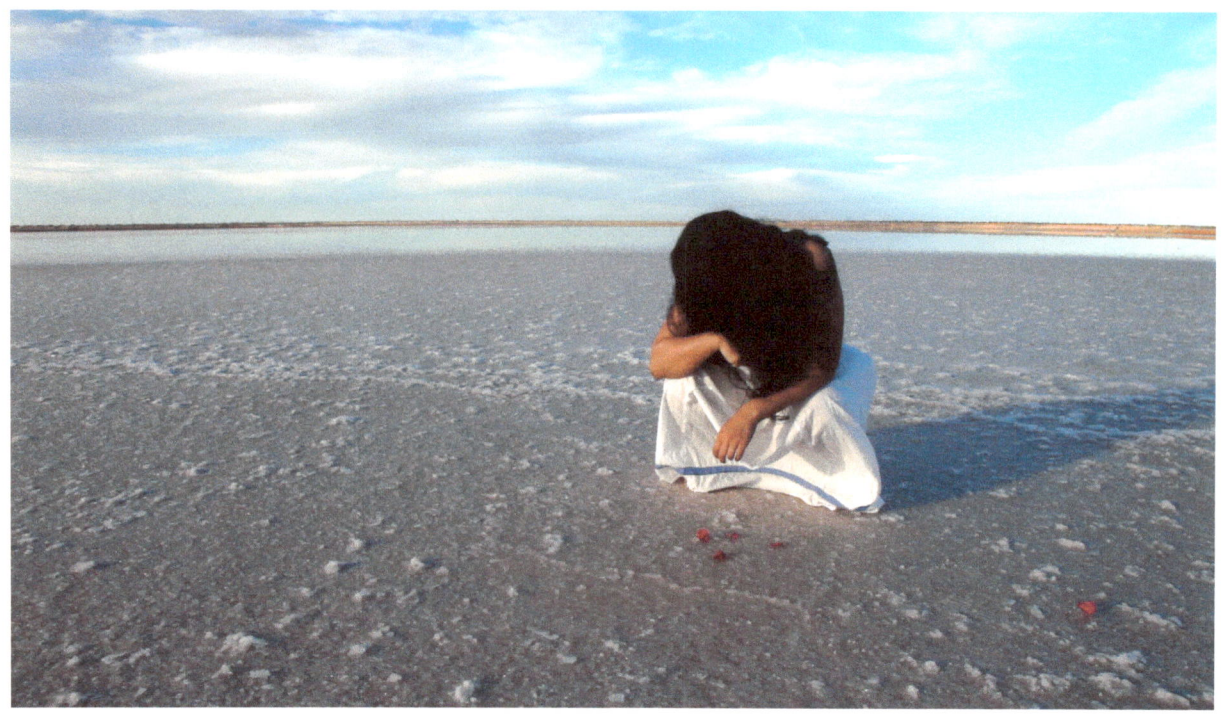

Gazelle Samizay, still from *Left*, 2011.

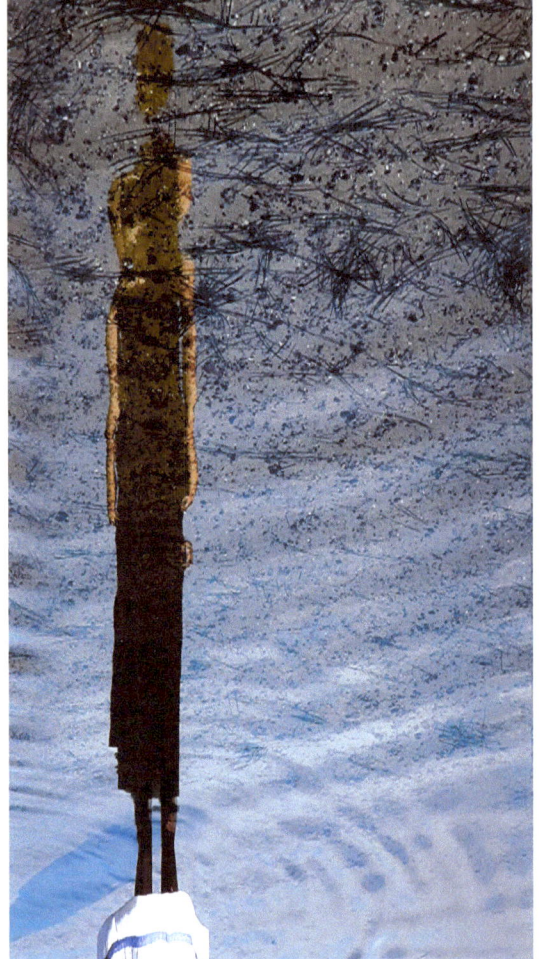

Gazelle Samizay, still from *im/pure*, 2011.

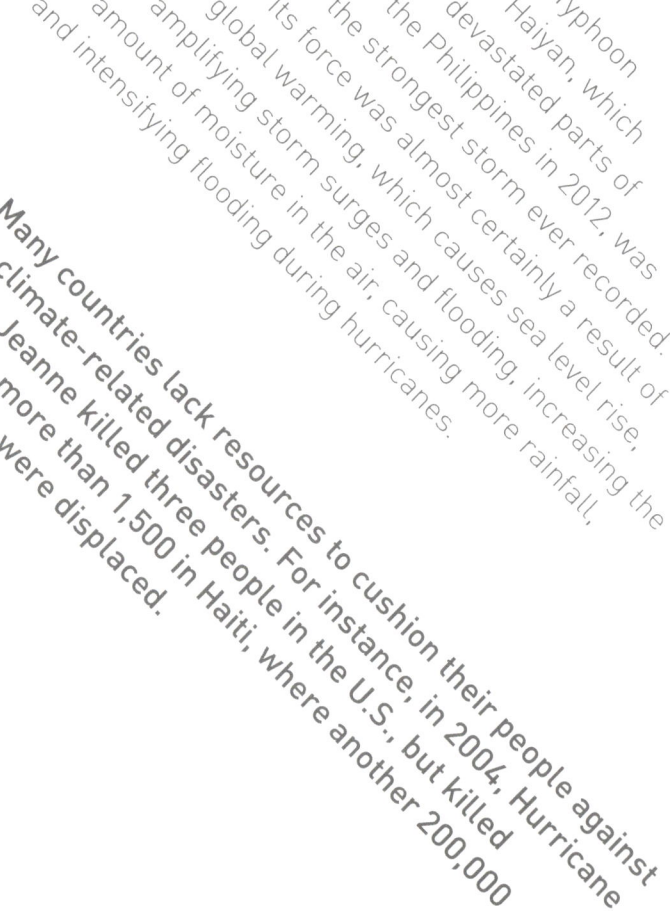

Typhoon Haiyan, which devastated parts of the Philippines in 2012, was the strongest storm ever recorded. Its force was almost certainly a result of global warming, which causes sea level rise, amplifying storm surges and flooding, increasing the amount of moisture in the air, causing more rainfall, and intensifying flooding during hurricanes.

Many countries lack resources to cushion their people against climate-related disasters. For instance, in 2004, Hurricane Jeanne killed three people in the U.S., but killed more than 1,500 in Haiti, where another 200,000 were displaced.

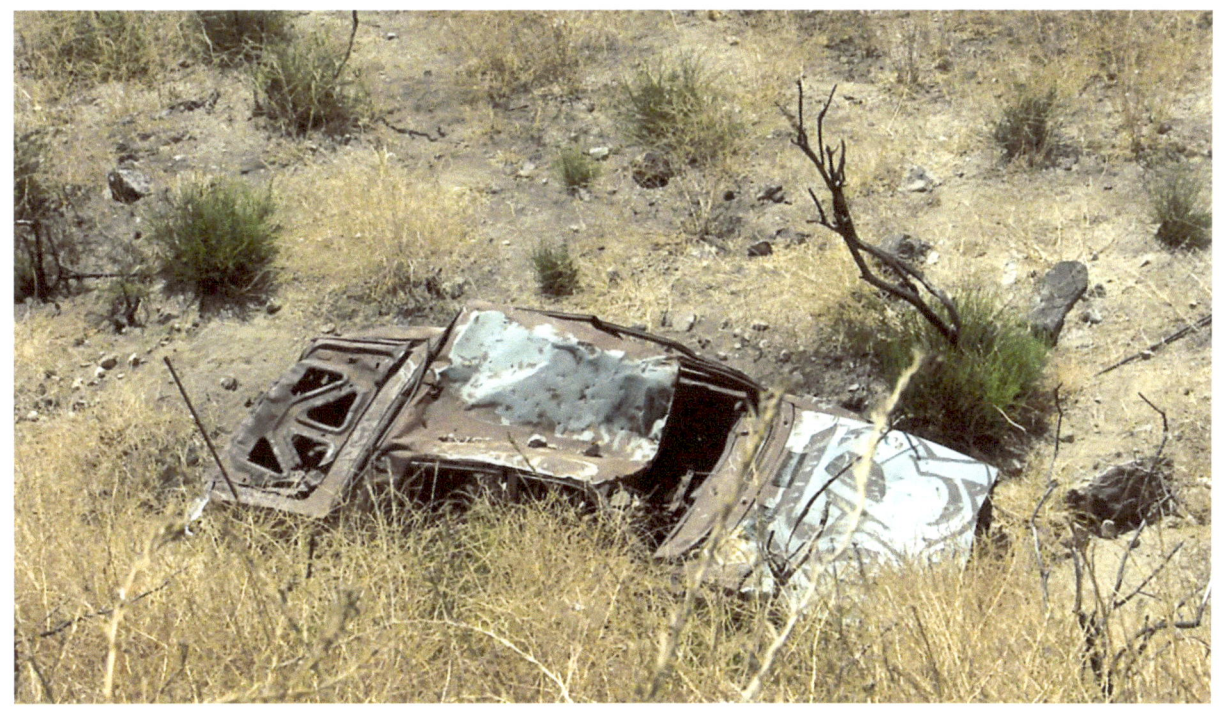

Beth Block, still from *Leaky Mountain*, undated.

Perth, Australia, could become the world's first "ghost metropolis," abandoned for lack of water. Similar fates await booming desert cities like Las Vegas, Phoenix, and Los Angeles. Large water diversions are expensive, inefficient, and environmentally destructive. Weather modification, such as cloud seeding, works in a limited fashion, but will not produce the necessary supply. Desalination of ocean water is costly and environmentally questionable. **Windhoek, Namibia, one of the driest places on Earth, relies solely on treated wastewater. In El Paso, Texas, 40% of tap water is recycled sewage.**

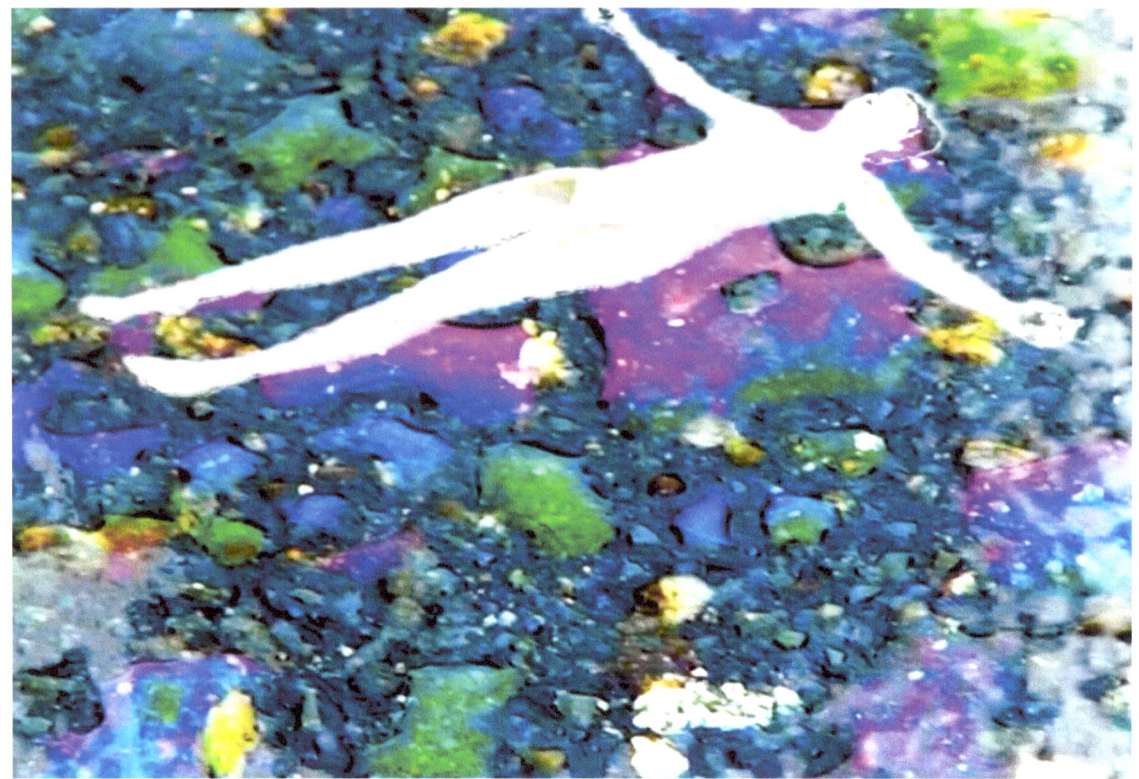

Krisanne Baker, still from *Upstream to Downstream (In Our Bloodstreams)*, undated.

Hydraulic fracturing, or "fracking," is the process of drilling and injecting fluid into the ground at high pressure to fracture shale rocks to release natural gas.

As many as 600 toxic and carcinogenic chemicals are used for fracking, such as uranium, mercury, ethylene glycol, hydrochloric acid, formaldehyde. Methane gas and toxic chemicals contaminate nearby groundwater.

TransCanada's Keystone XL pipeline would slice through America's agricultural heartland, the Missouri, Platte, and Niobrara Rivers, the Ogallala aquifer, habitat for sage grouse and sandhill cranes, walleye fisheries, croplands, and much more. Our public water supplies will all be at risk of dangerous tar sands oil spills like the million-gallon 2010 Enbridge oil spill in Michigan.

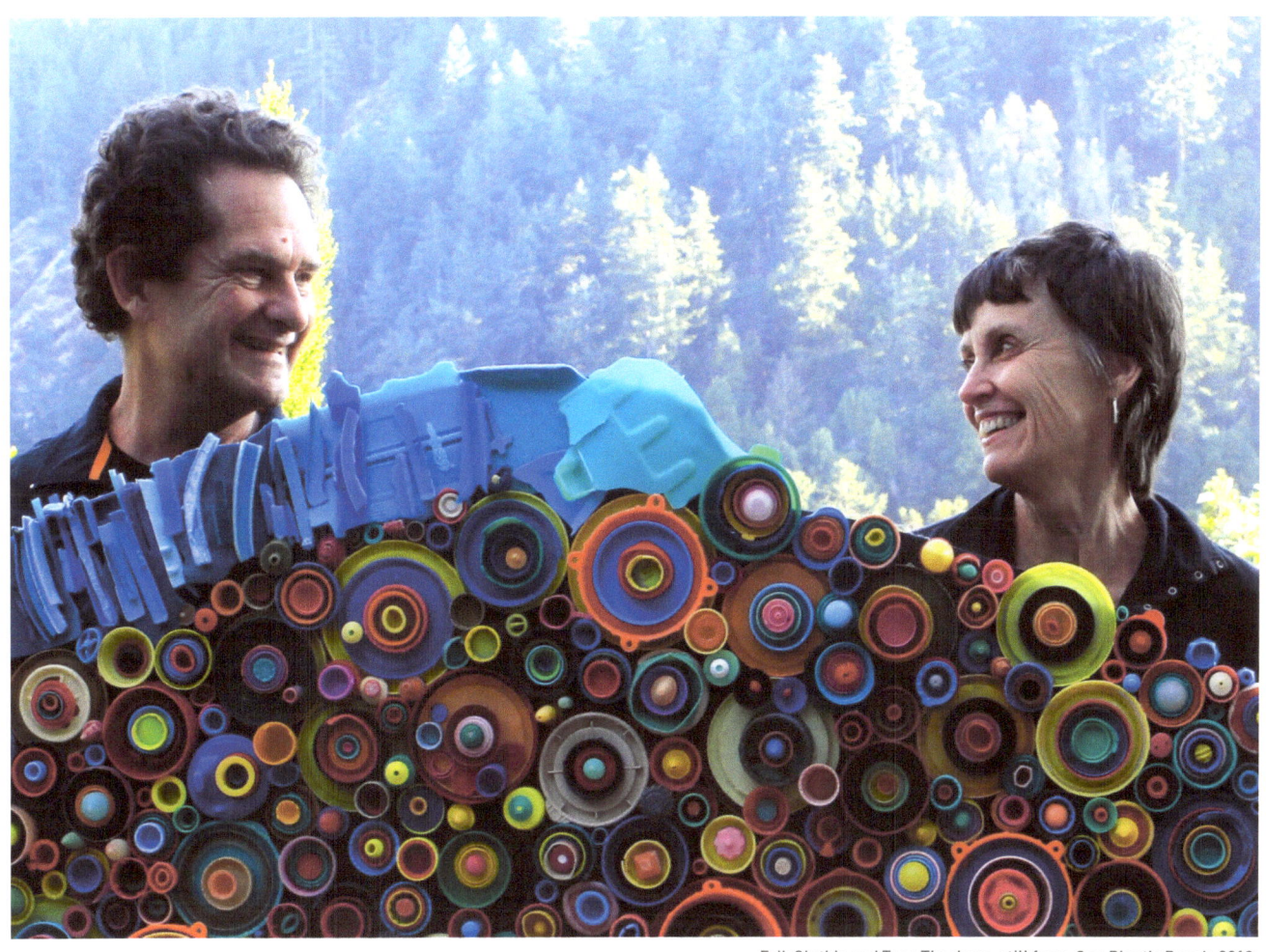

Erik Slatkin and Tess Thackara, still from *One Plastic Beach*, 2010.

It takes 1 to 8 million gallons of water to complete each fracking job.

Each gas well requires an average of 400 tanker trucks to carry water and supplies to and from the site.

500,000 active wells in the United States x 8 million gallons of water per fracking x 18 times a well can be fracked = 7 trillion gallons of water.

43

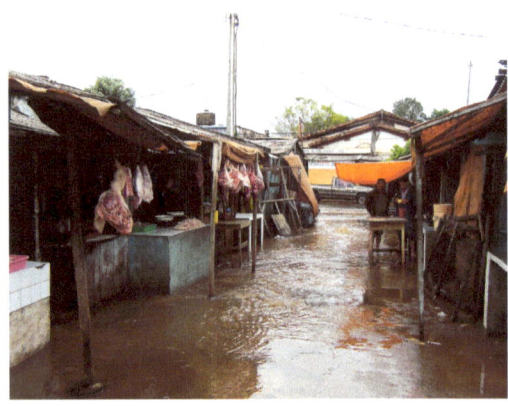

Carla Pataky and International Rivers, still from *A River Runs Through Us*, 2010.

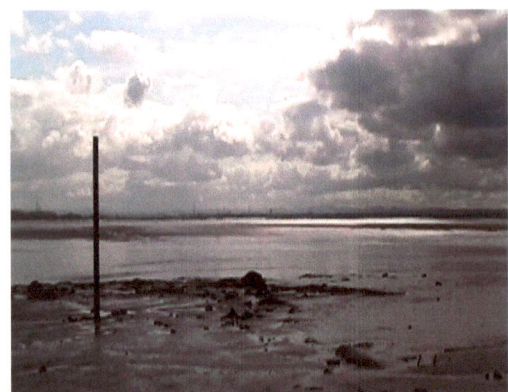

James Brady, still from *Floodland Study #1*, 2009.

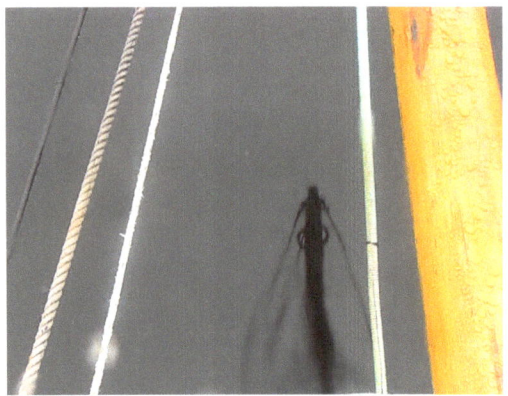

Pat Law, still from *Voyage*, 2010.

The 2011 Fukushima Daiichi nuclear disaster in Japan was caused by the Tohoku earthquake and tsunami and was the largest nuclear incident since the Chernobyl disaster in 1986.

The Fukushima disaster displaced 50,000 households after radioactive material leaked into the air, soil, and sea. Radiation checks led to bans on some shipments of vegetables and fish.

There have been over 1,000 documented cases of water contamination next to areas of gas drilling, as well as cases of sensory, respiratory, and neurological damage due to ingested contaminated water.

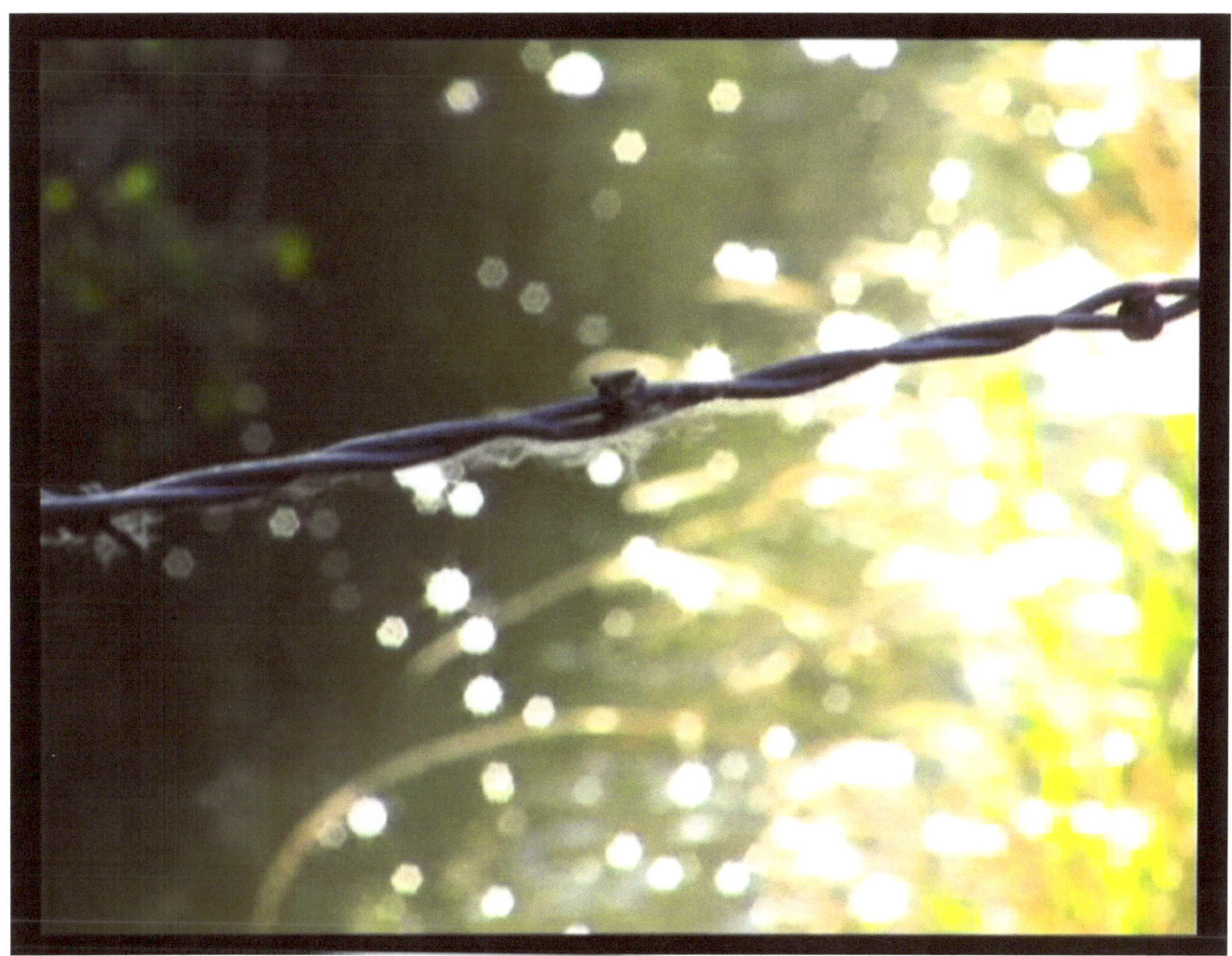

J. Gluckstern, still from *Ditches of Boulder*, 2009.

"The Earth's surface is 71% covered in water, and water is the primary force shaping every element of the character of the planet – the geology, the weather, the range and variety of life, the planet's gleaming profile in space..."

– Charles Fishman, *The Big Thirst: The Secret Life and Turbulent Future of Water*, 2011

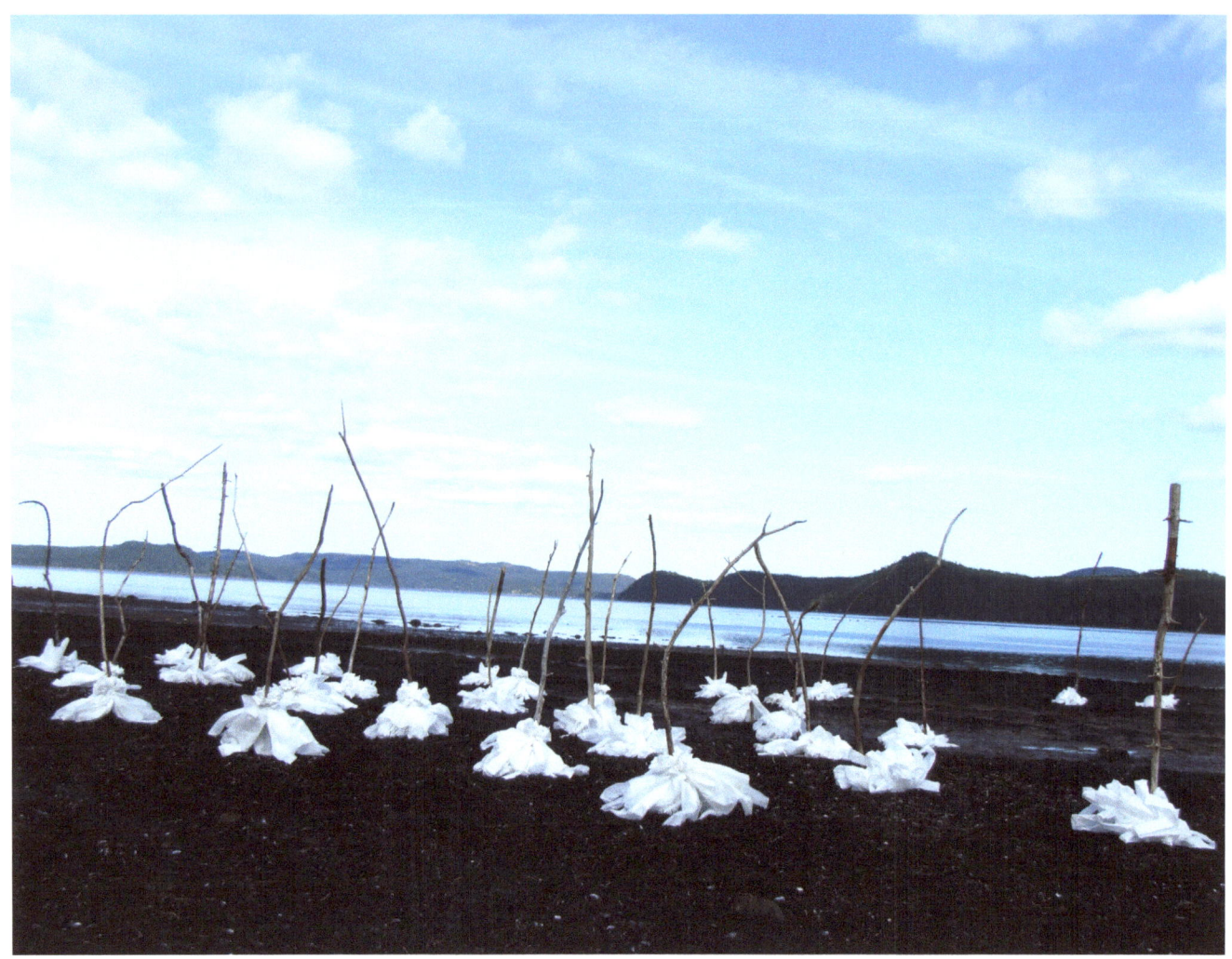

Claudia Borgna, still from *Poise of Tides*, 2010.

In the U.S., more than 30 billion plastic water bottles are discarded each year. Only 15% are recycled; the rest end up in landfills, or as litter – 66 million every day. They can take 1,000 years to decompose. Meanwhile, they contribute to the vortex of plastic waste in the Pacific Garbage Patch.

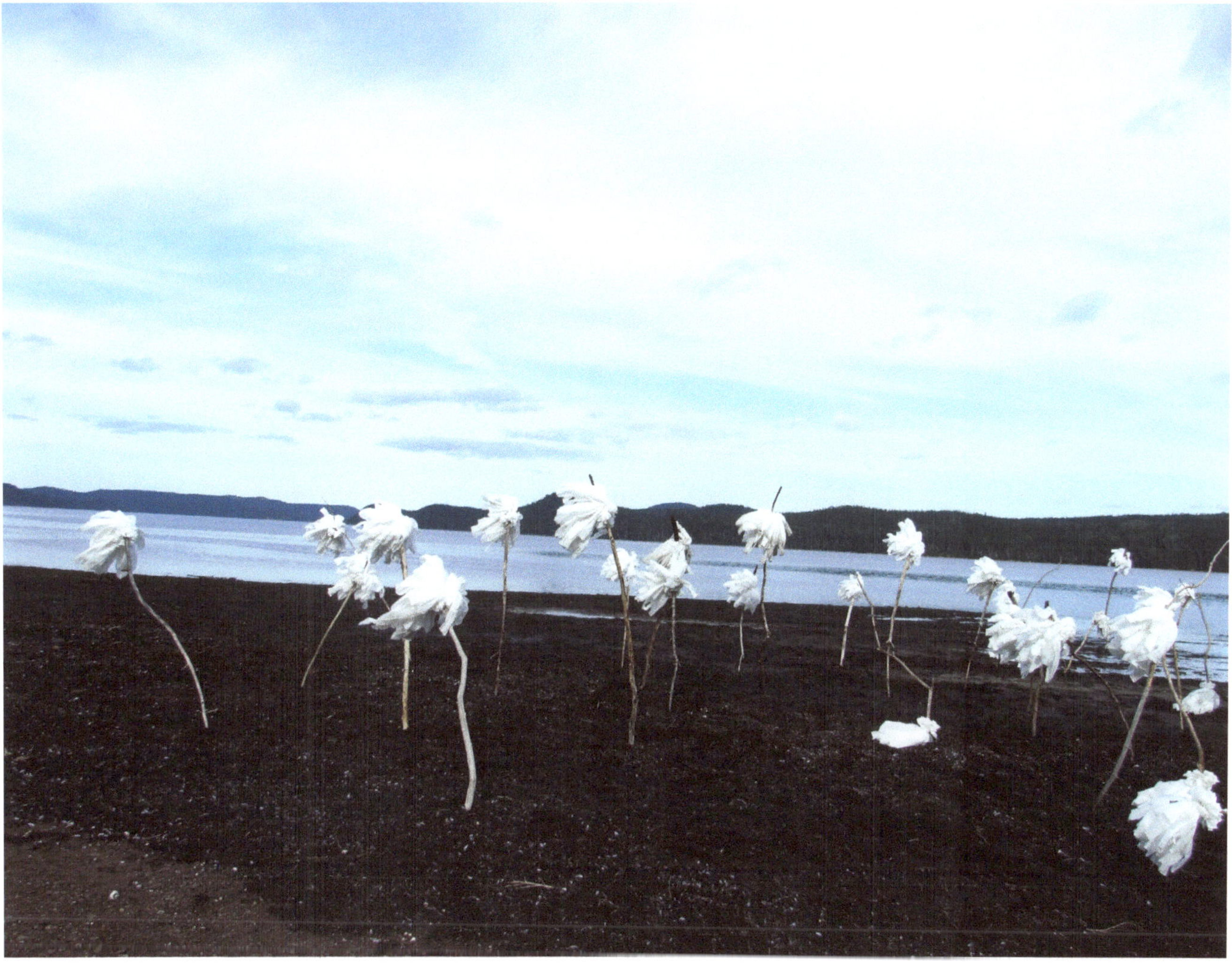

Claudia Borgna, still from *Sweep & Weep, Weep & Sweep*, 2010.

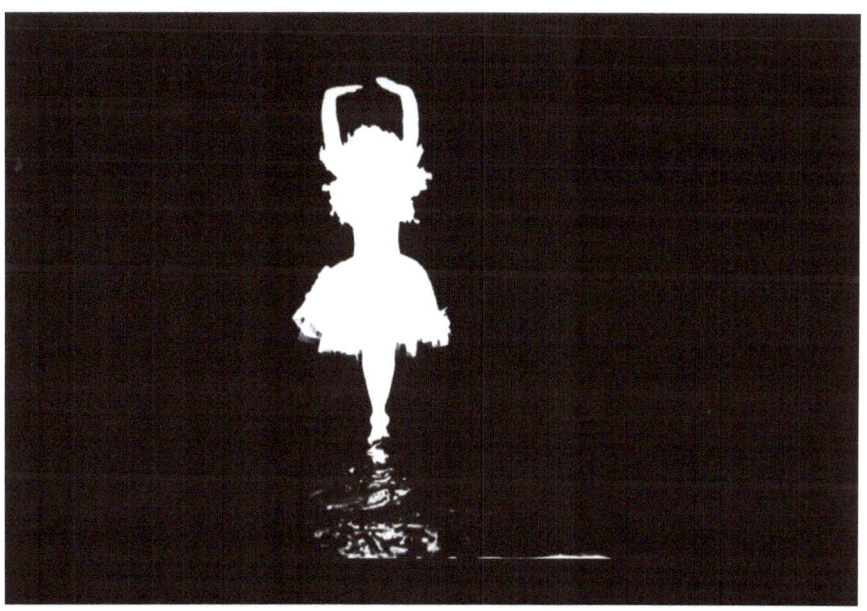

Fiammetta de Michele, still from *Louisiana*, undated.

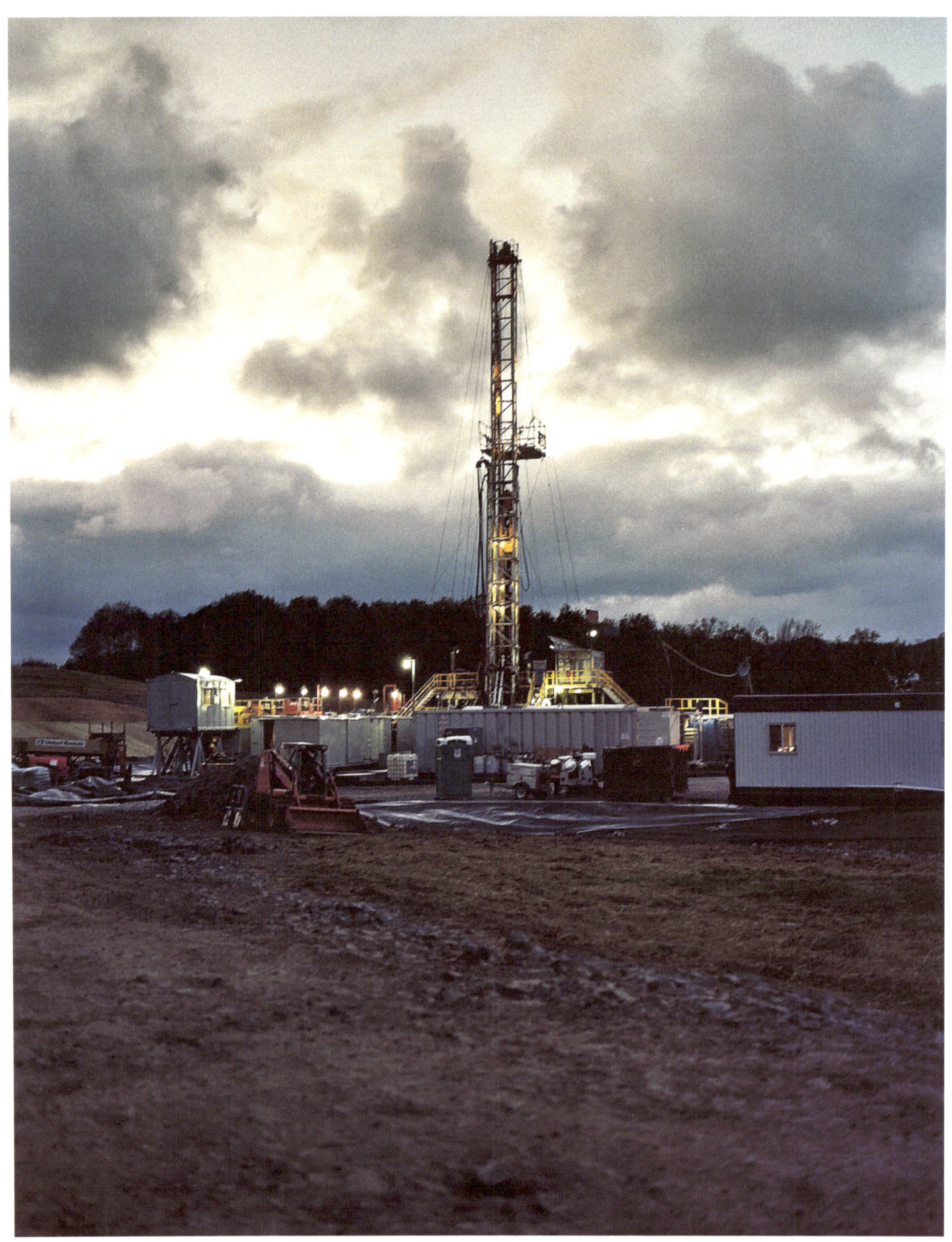

Jacques de Conte, still from *A Colossal Fracking Mess*, 2010.

Drought can occur in any climate, arid or humid.

As the world's human population increases, the burden on Earth's water supply increases.

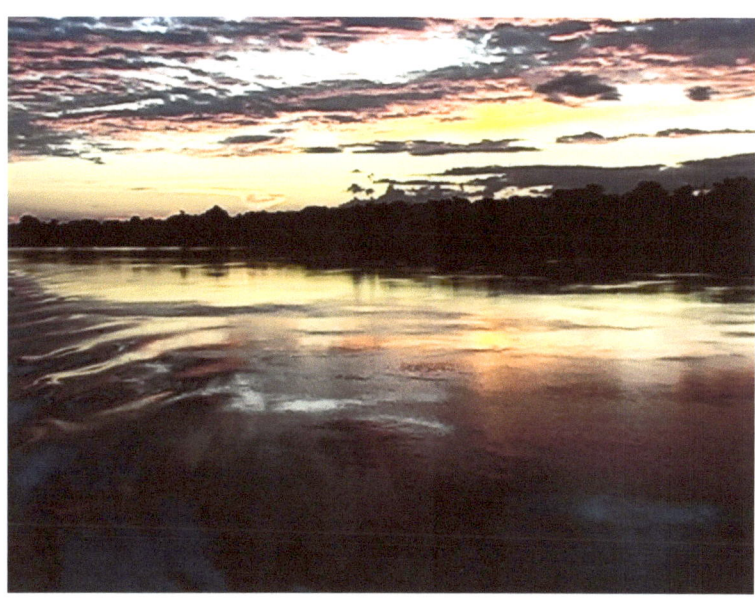

Christine Baeumler, still from *Amazon Twilight*, 2010.

By 2025, global demand for water will increase by two-thirds more than the demand in 2013.

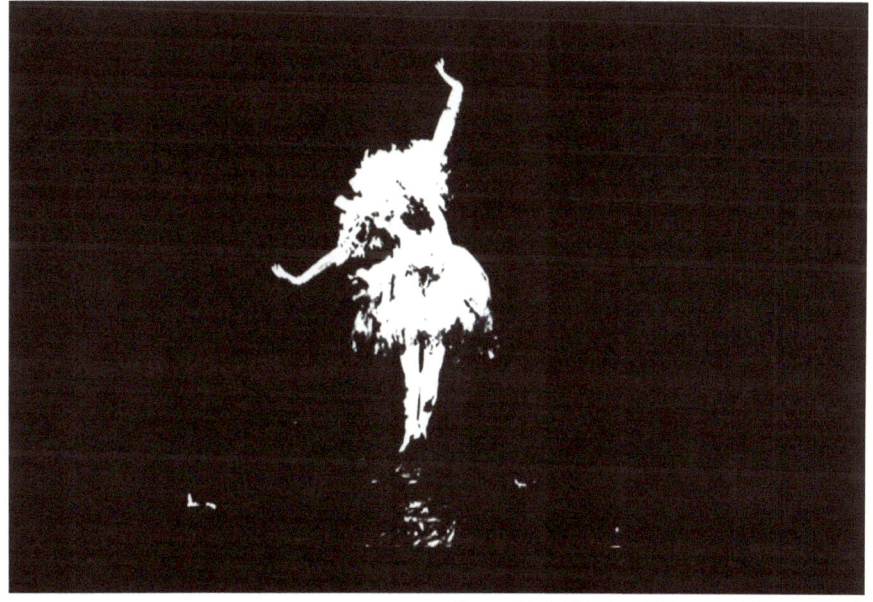

Fiammetta de Michele, still from *Louisiana*, undated.

Only .003% of Earth's fresh water is not polluted, trapped in soil, or too far underground to reach. During a drought, shared sources of water such as reservoirs, rivers, and groundwater for wells are in jeopardy of running dry.

The Great Pacific Garbage Patch is a gyre of marine litter in the central North Pacific Ocean extending over a large, but indeterminate, area. It is characterized by exceptionally high concentrations of pelagic plastics, chemical sludge, and other debris that end up in the stomachs of marine birds and animals. This toxin-containing plastic is also eaten by jellyfish, which are then eaten by larger fish, which are eaten by humans.

Droughts are a gradual deficiency of precipitation that in severe cases can last for many years and have devastating effects on agriculture and water supplies.

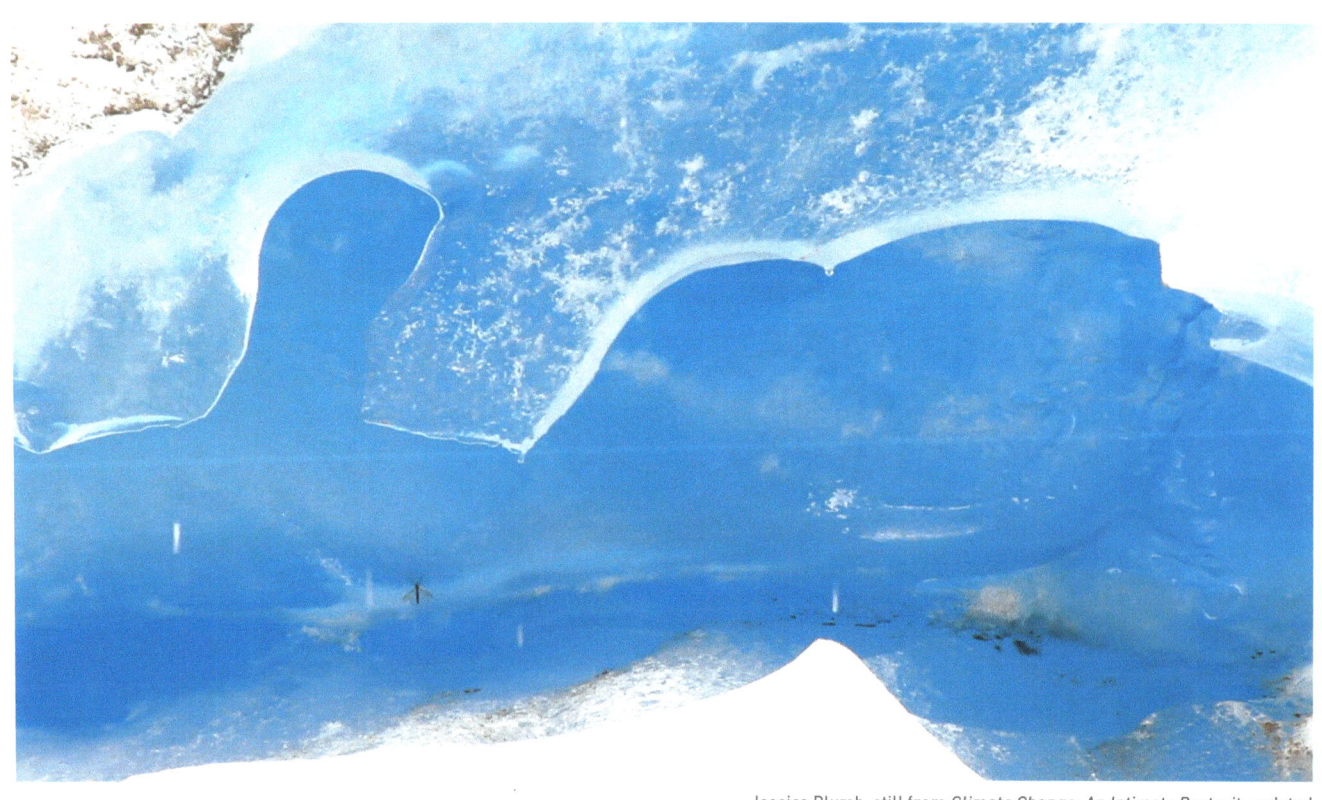

Jessica Plumb, still from *Climate Change: An Intimate Portrait*, undated

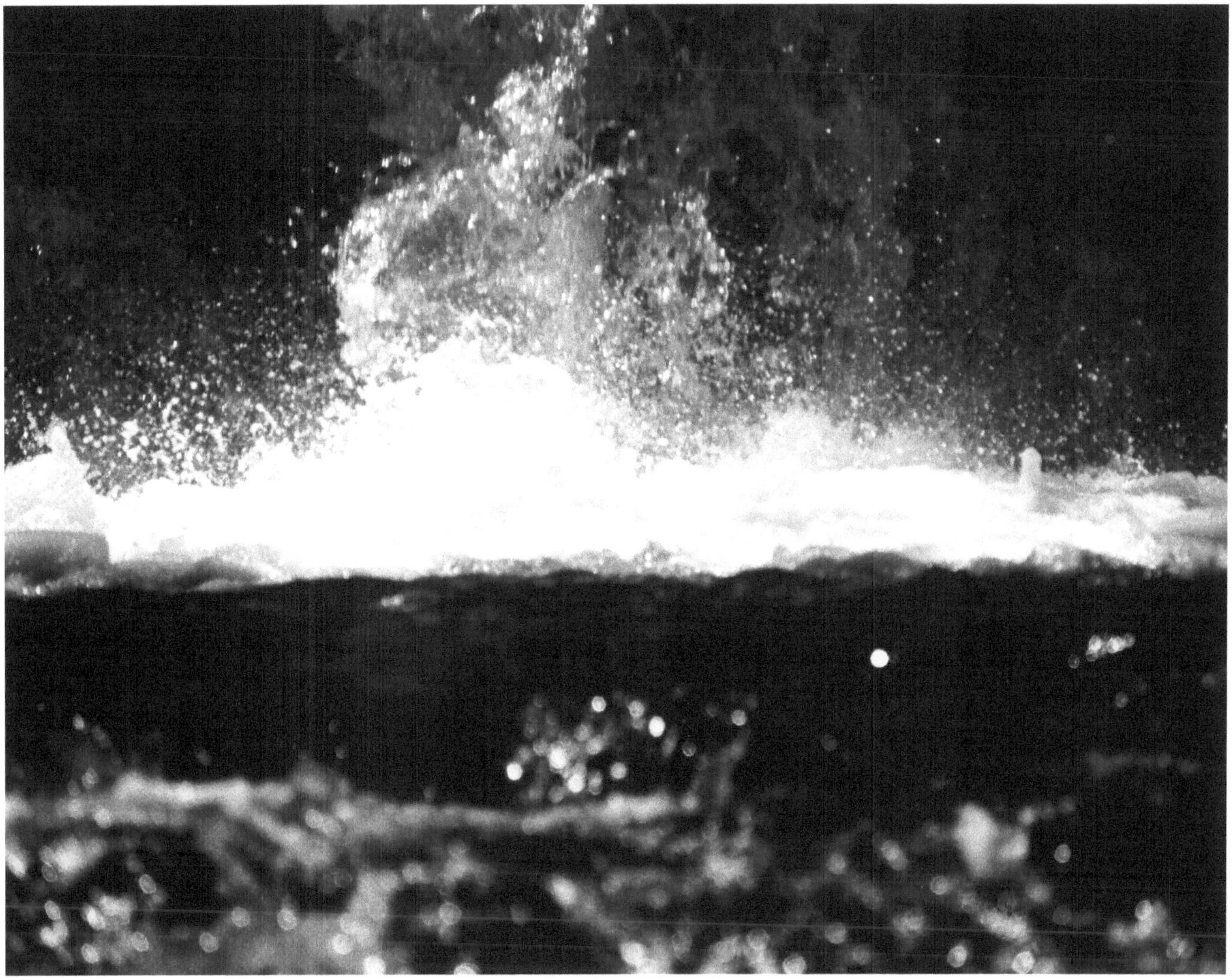

Liz Marshall, still from *Excerpt from Water on the Table*, 2010.

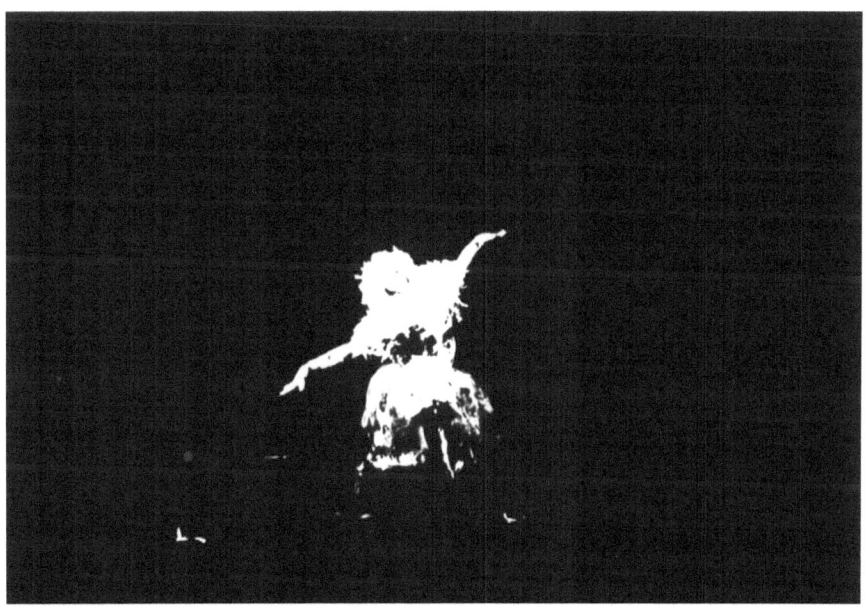

Fiammetta de Michele, still from *Louisiana*, undated.

Still Life with Water Glass

Mercury, silver, lead of course, selenium and chlorine,

DDT, dioxins, PCBs,

The harmless (or not so harmless) fluorides,

Freon from a cast-off Frigidaire,

Sulfuric acid, sulfate, sulfites too in phantom traces,

Admixed to a spectral base

Of cellophane and fluorocarbons

From fifty million hair-spray cans a year

All dance together in a dark conjunction,

Spin tonight without even a ripple

Treading with me to your bedside table,

Who brought this glass while you were fast asleep.

— Michael Wolfe

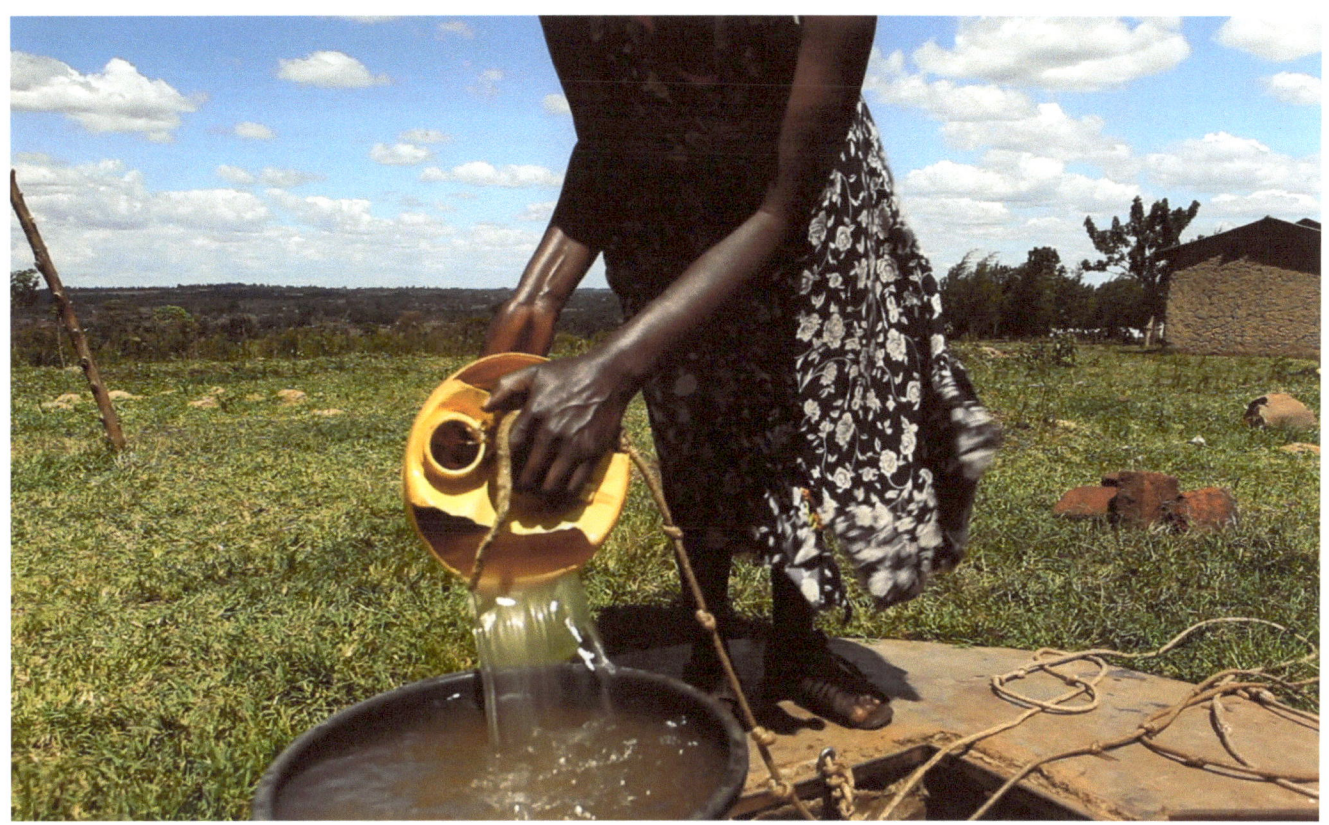

Evan Abramson and Carmen Elsa Lopez, still from *Carbon for Water*, 2011.

War is inherently destructive to the environment. Air, water, and soil are polluted, humans and animals are killed, and numerous health effects occur among the living.

In the Horn of Africa, the 1984–1985 drought led to a famine that killed 750,000 people.

Almost 4 million people die each year from water-related diseases.

In a five-year period, chemical factories, manufacturing plants, and other workplaces in the United States violated water pollution laws more than half a million times. The violations ranged from failing to report emissions to dumping toxins at concentrations that regulators say might contribute to cancer, birth defects, and other illnesses.

Human activity such as dams, river regulation measures, intensified land use and forestry, as well as emissions of greenhouse gases are triggering or worsening floods in Europe and the United States, as evidenced by the levees in and around New Orleans, which attempted to reroute water from Lake Pontchartrain, the Mississippi River, and the nearby Gulf of Mexico. They failed to protect the city, worsening the flooding caused by Hurricane Katrina in 2005.

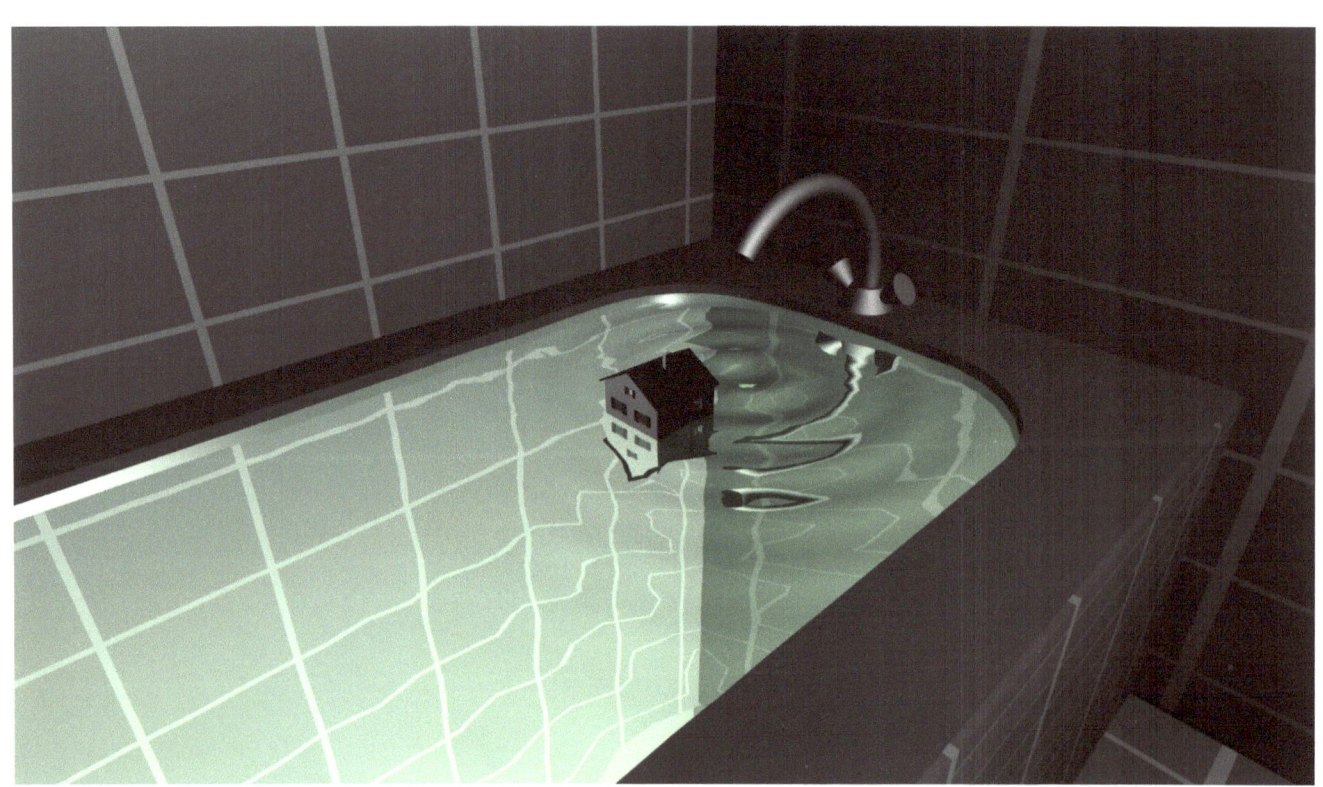

Susanne Wiegner, still from *Constant Dripping or No Escape*, 2009.

THIS BROOK – CALLED BY THE DUTCH, BESTAVAAR'S KILL, AND BY THE ENGLISH, MANETTA WATER ... ALTHOUGH NO LONGER VISIBLE ... FLOWS IN DIMINISHED VOLUME IN ITS OLD CHANNEL

The hurrying in streaks
Bank rivulets one origin known

Charter and lay little ever(y) day
Beloved yellow
That hidden evidence
Deep Union thence curving hostilities

By eastern spring thence and vicinity and Amity ran single
Known its later letters

As no degradations
Before yellow
These here evidence
Eye no graveyard lost it's still heavy

Memory almost numerous east to the across
Without about turning east ran

A little they here outside under glowing Hill
No one
Levelled only new growth early river
Visible immediately set it below luck extended
Occupied lived during
Citizen honored always now number earth lay

– E.J. McAdams

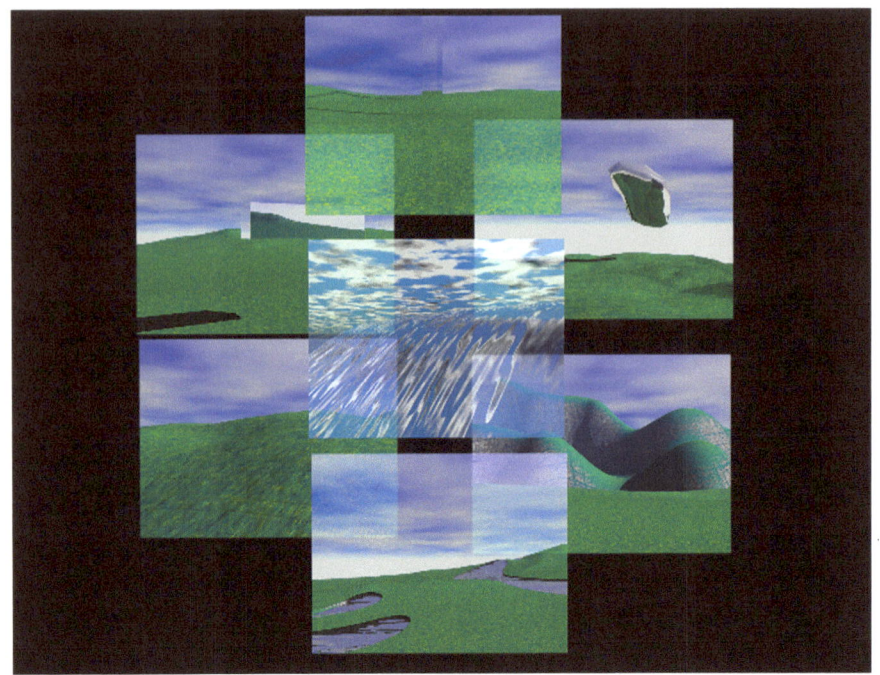

Henry Gwiazda, still from *there's whispering*, 2003.

The Freedom Industries site behind the 2014 West Virginia chemical spill is just a mile upriver from the state's largest water treatment plant, owned by American Water. More than 16% of West Virginia's residents' water supply was compromised and the environment is likely forever poisoned.

Environmental inspectors had not visited West Virginia's Freedom Industries facility since 1991.

Currently there is a rush to privatize water services around the world. Private companies often violate standards of operation, and engage in price fixing without many consequences. This leads to water stress among poor populations, often causing people to drink water that is often contaminated.

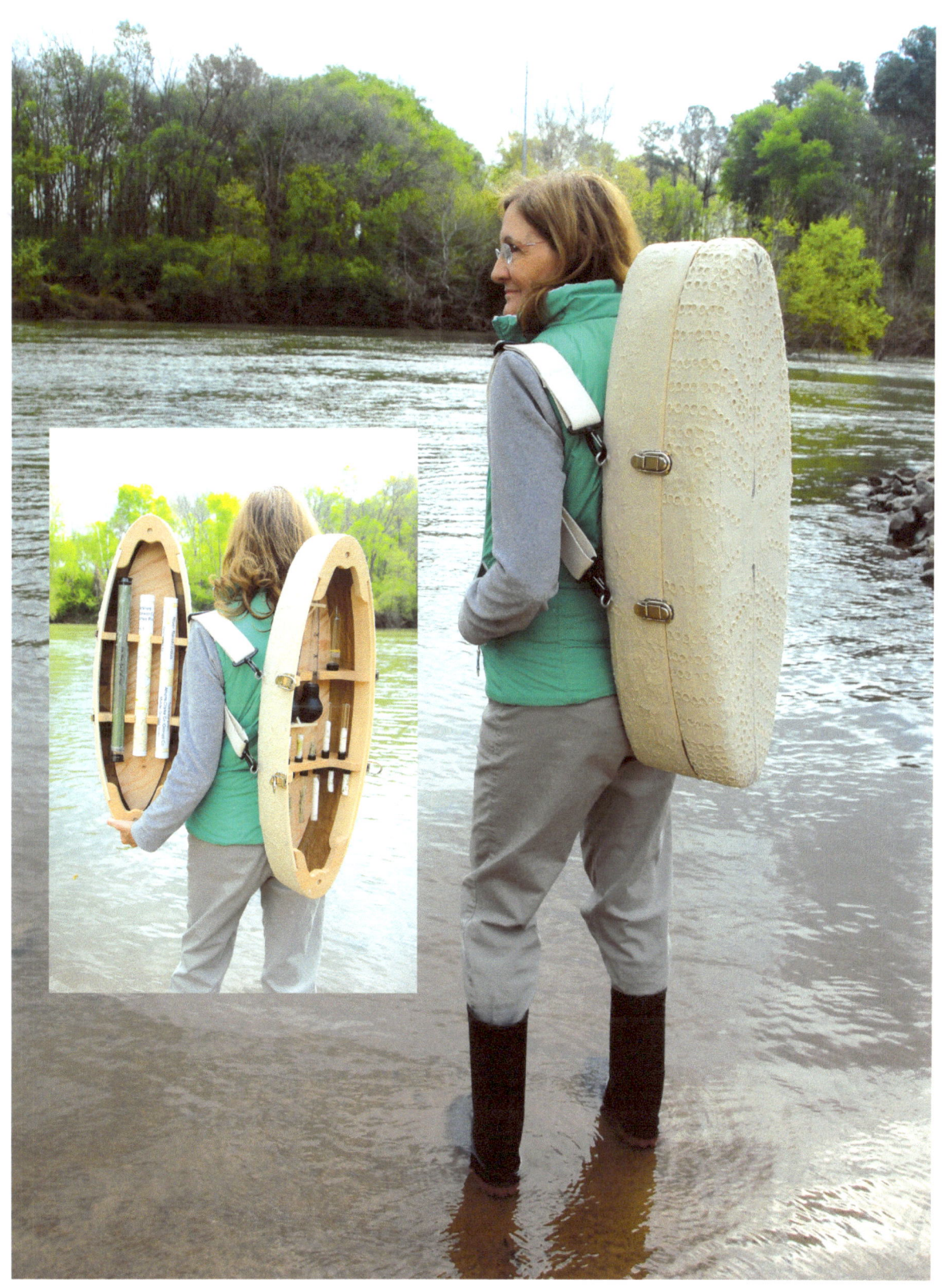

Basia Irland, still from *A Gathering of Waters*, 1999.

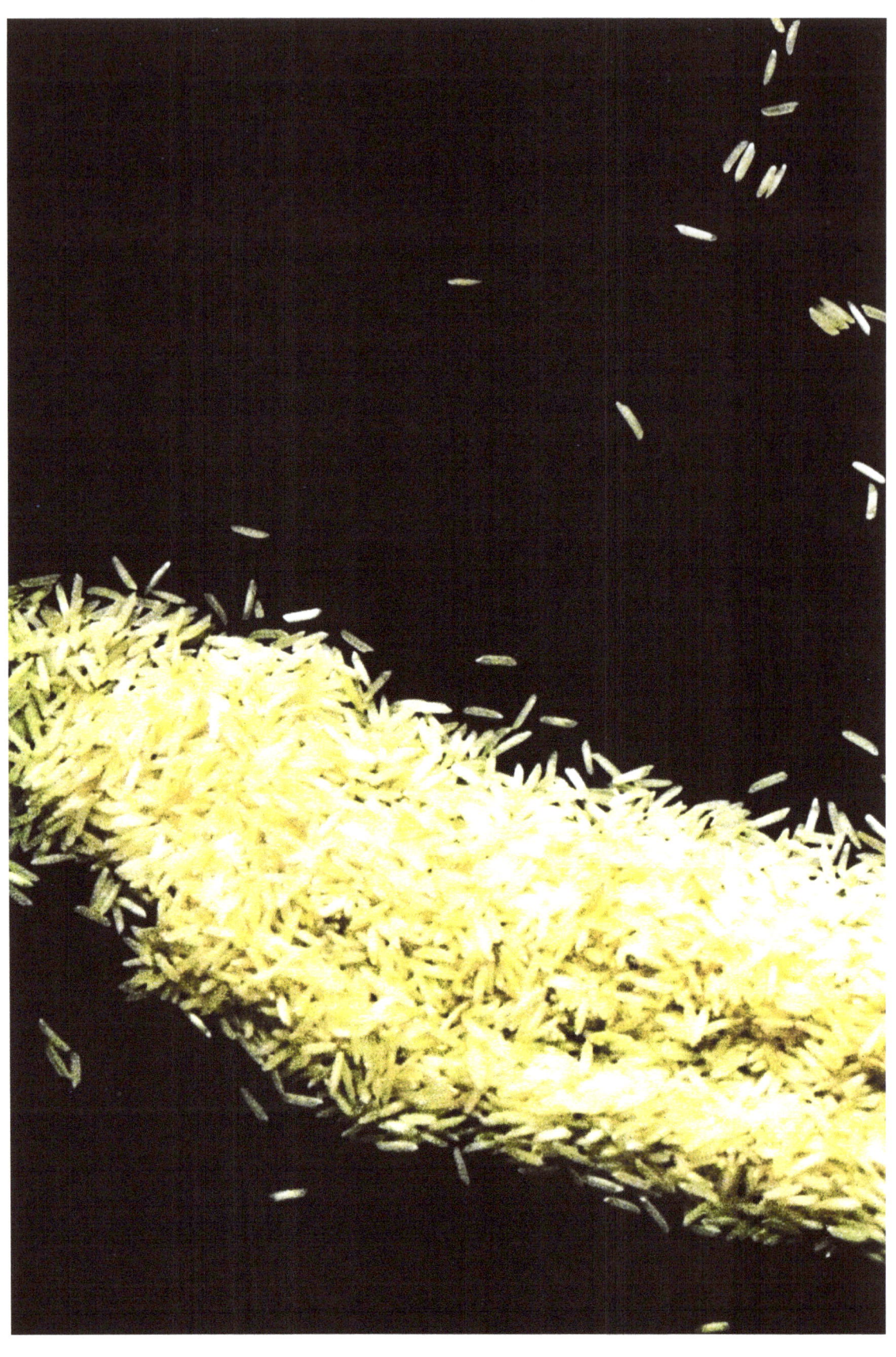

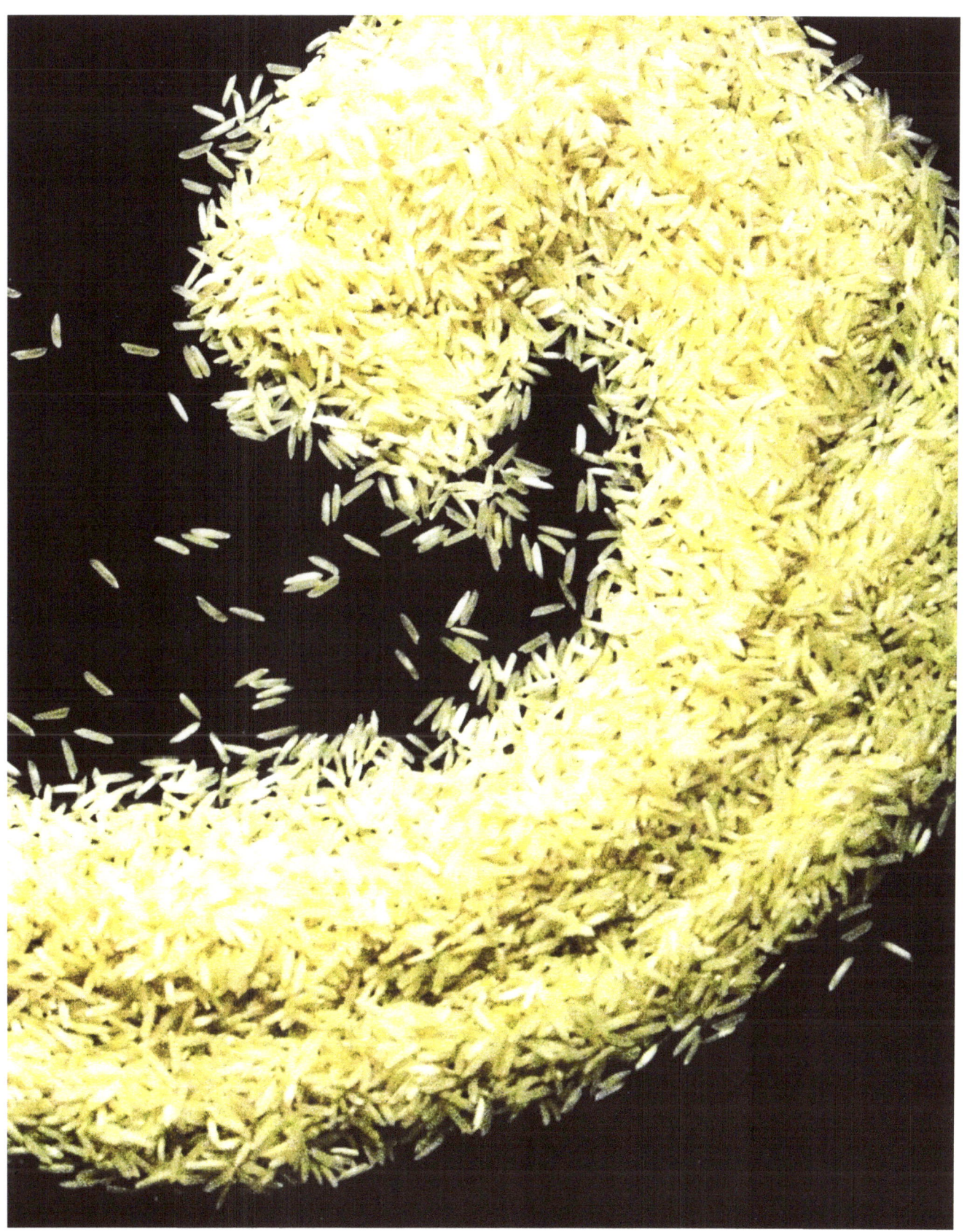

Carolyn Radlo and Alanna Simone, still from *Rice Relief*, 2009/2011.

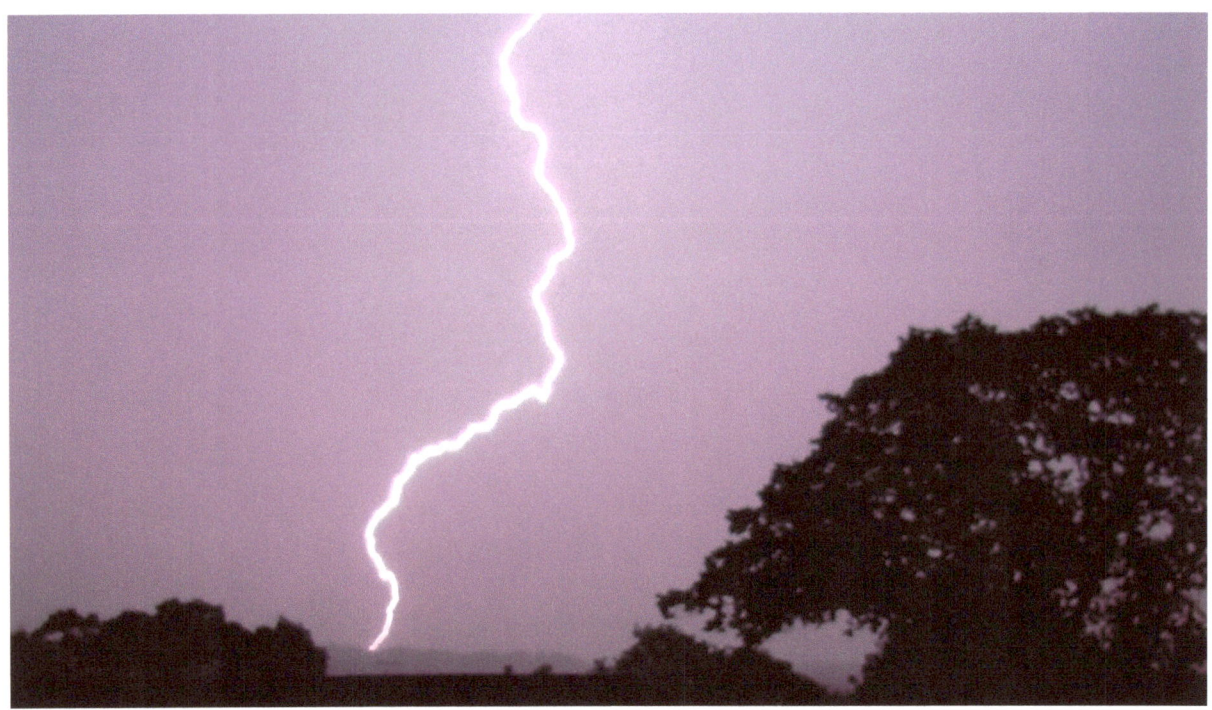

Georgie Friedman, still from *Light of the Storm*, 2011.

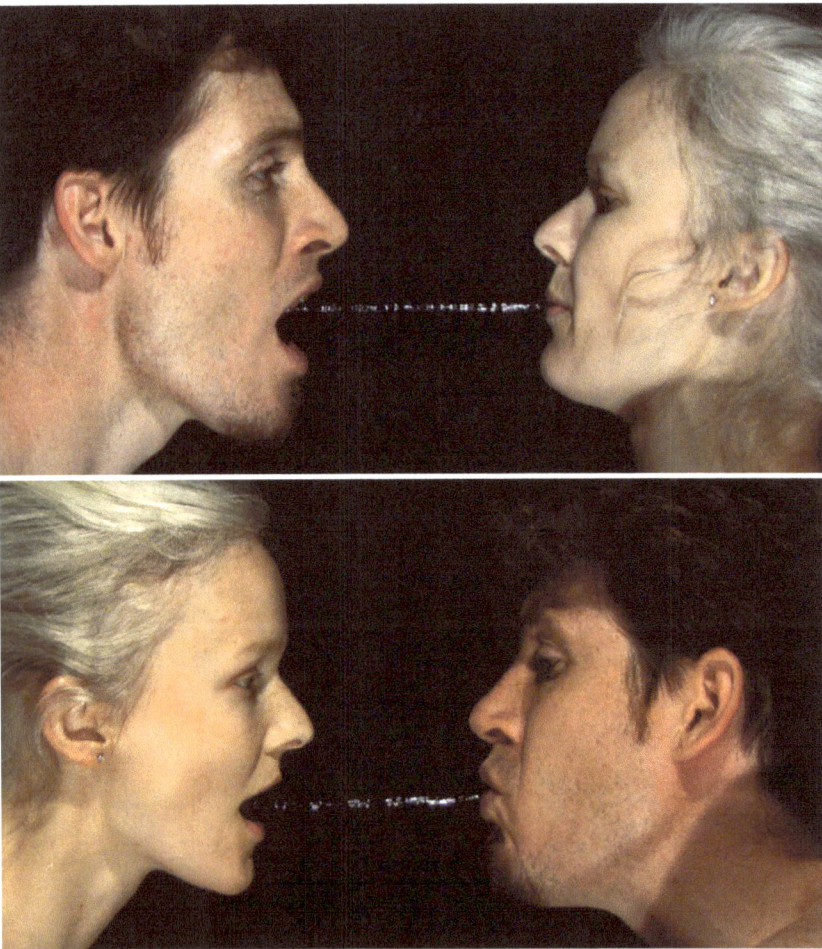

Robert Ladislas Derr, stills from *Conservation of Momentum*, 2009.

The vast majority of polluters escape unpunished, as state officials repeatedly ignore obvious illegal dumping, and the Environmental Protection Agency, which, thanks to the Clean Water Act (passed by Congress in 1972), can prosecute polluters when states fail to act, has often declined to intervene.

Millions of people live in areas increasingly vulnerable to flooding, forcing them to abandon their homes and relocate. Low-lying islands could be submerged completely.

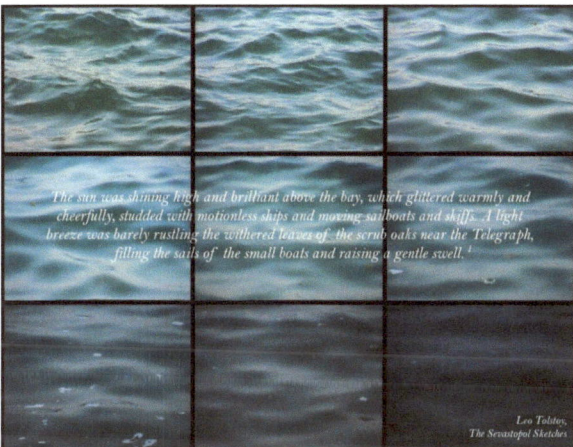

Tobias Rosenberger, still from *Sevastopol in August*, undated.

Countries like Bangladesh, Kiribati, and the Maldives are in immediate and critical danger.

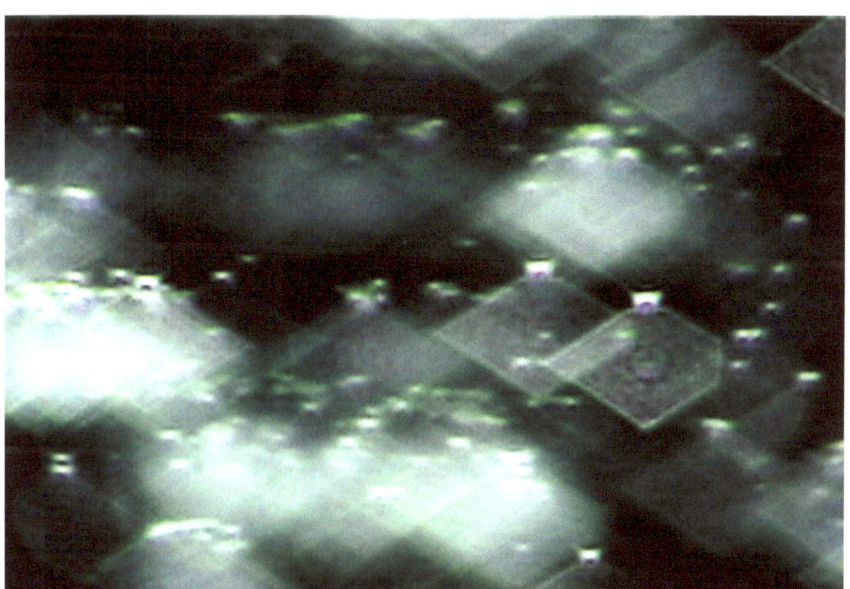

Diane Armitage, still from *The Great River*, 2002.

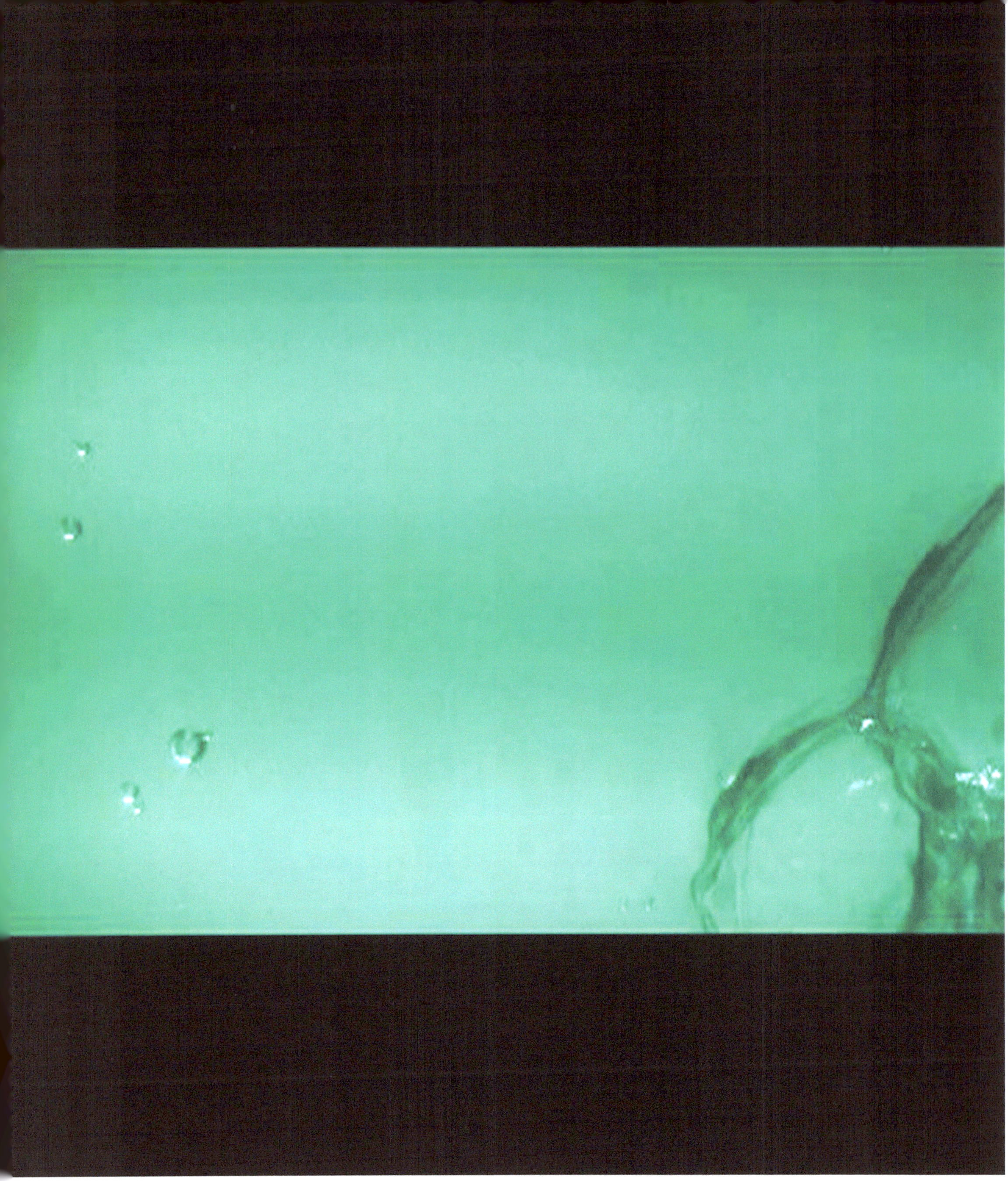

"Once we kill the coral reefs and the rain forest, this Earth is toast."

– Michael Berryman, American actor

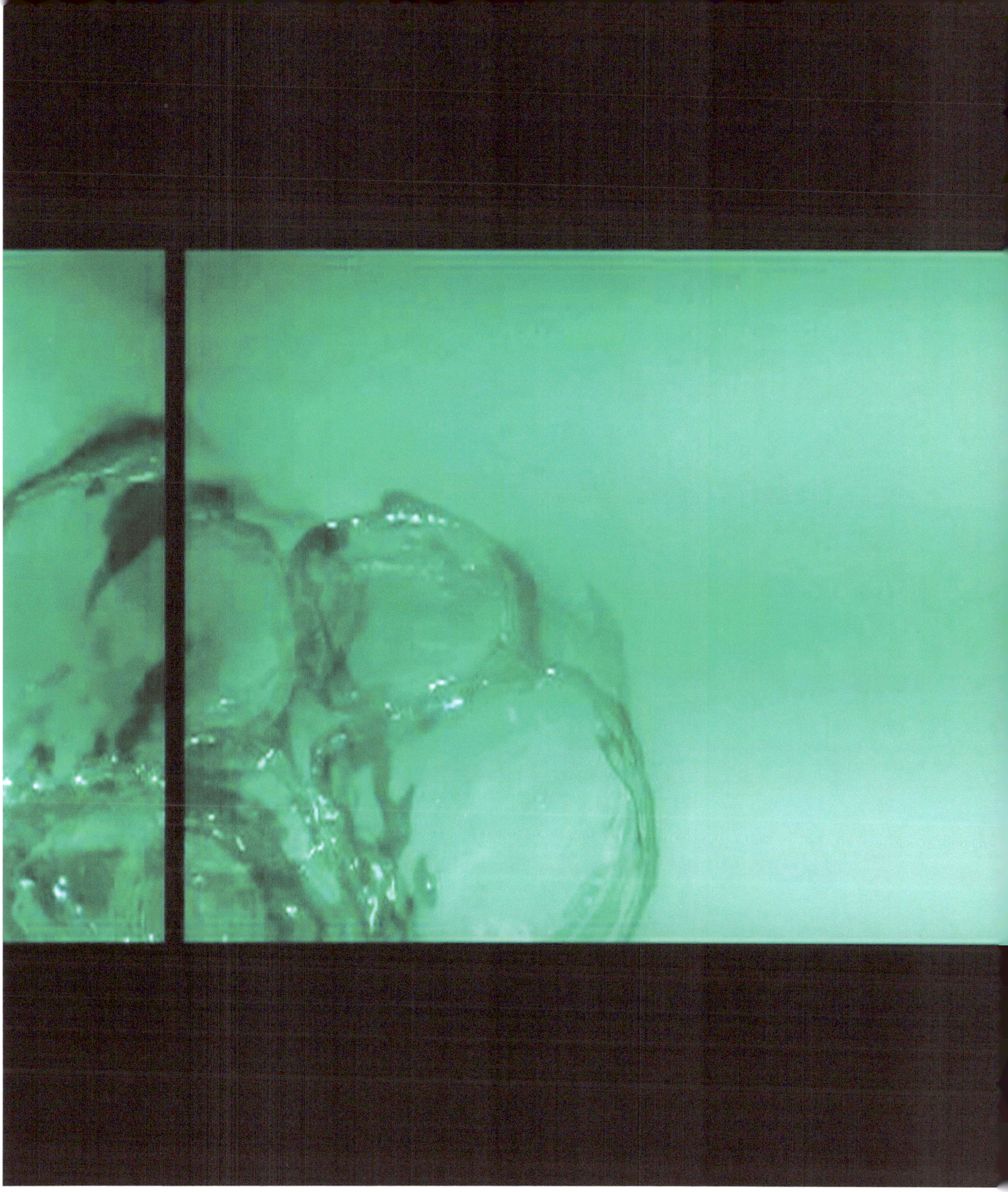

Patrizia Monzani, still from *found footage*, 2006.

Tar sands extraction causes enormous ecological destruction, beginning with clear cutting the boreal forest, then strip-mined. The subsoil is destroying habitat and soil. The waste tailings are toxic slurry that penetrates groundwater and wells. As with "fracking," vast quantities of water are needed for the tar sands industry.

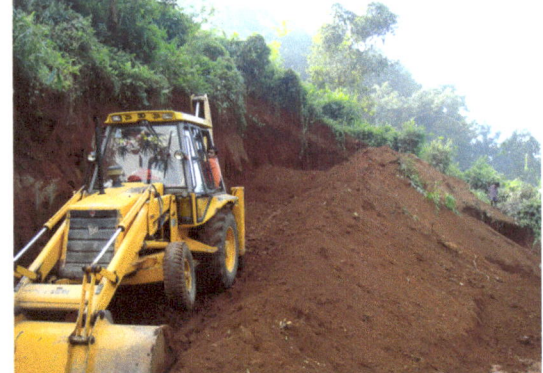

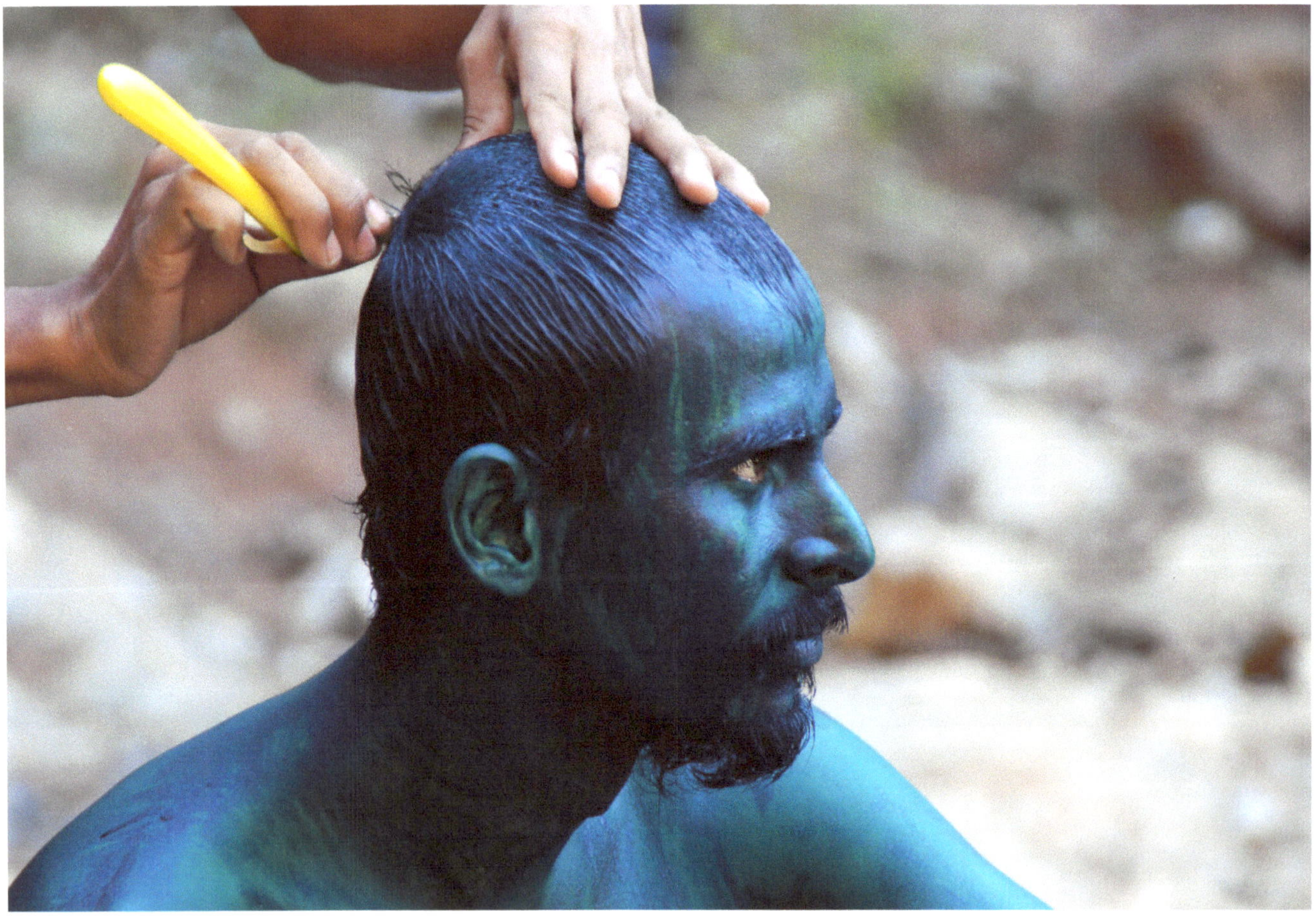

Manoj Baviskar, stills from *I Came... I Saw... Prayed for Someone Whom I love*, 2008.

Tar sands are low-grade hydrocarbon deposits that require enormous energy input to process and convert them into something resembling petroleum.

In the United States, drought can have major impacts on agriculture, recreation and tourism, reserve water supply, forest and wildland fires, energy production, and transportation. Nationwide losses from the U.S. drought of 1988, for example, exceeded $40 billion.

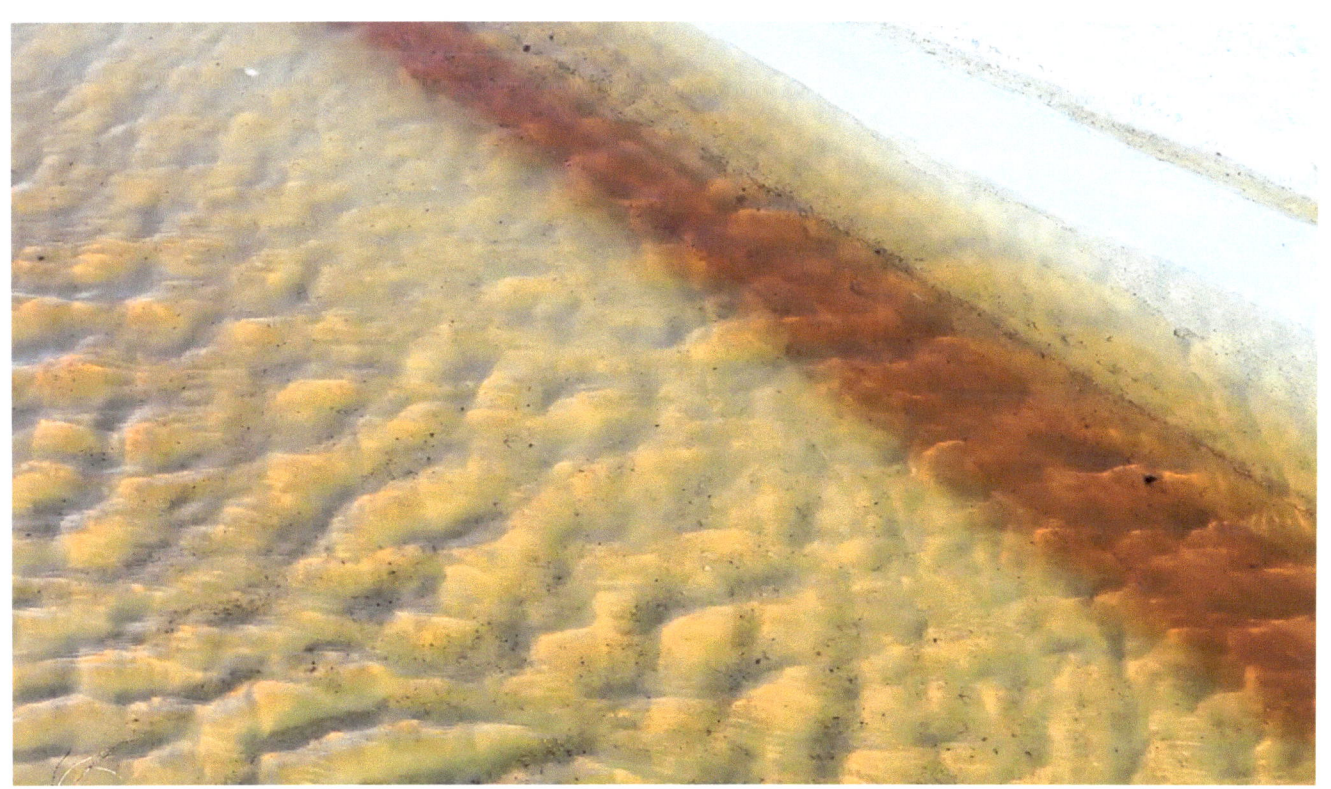

Jason Houston, still from *Indonesian Borneo: Water Meditation*, 2009.

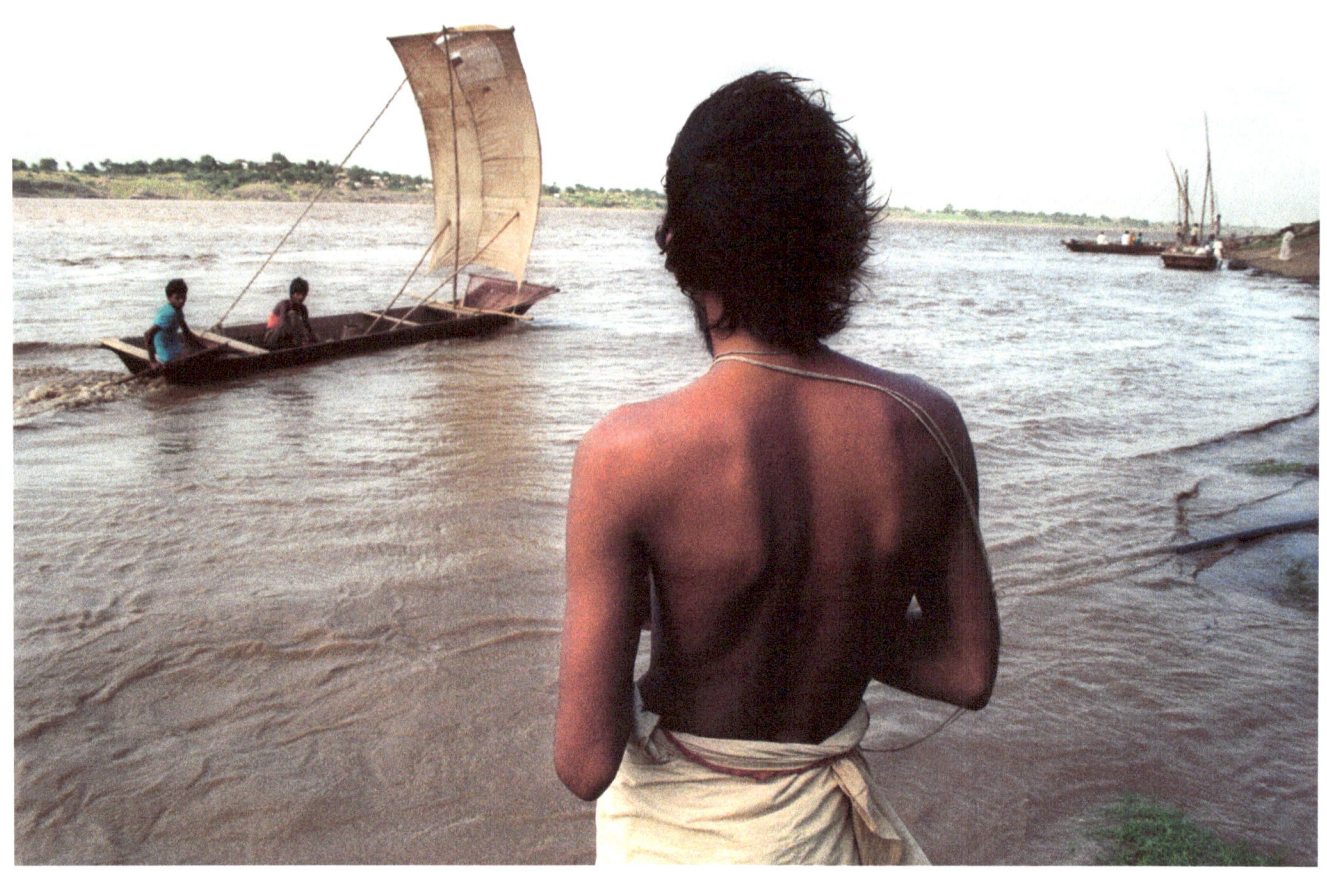

Carla Pataky and International Rivers, still from *A River Runs Through Us*, 2010.

In 2006, it was estimated that worldwide there are 25 to 50 million climate refugees (also known as "environmental migrants") due to drought, flooding, hurricanes, or heat waves, with predictions of many more displaced peoples to come.

It takes 60 pounds of water to produce 1 pound of potatoes and 168 pounds to produce 1 pound of corn.

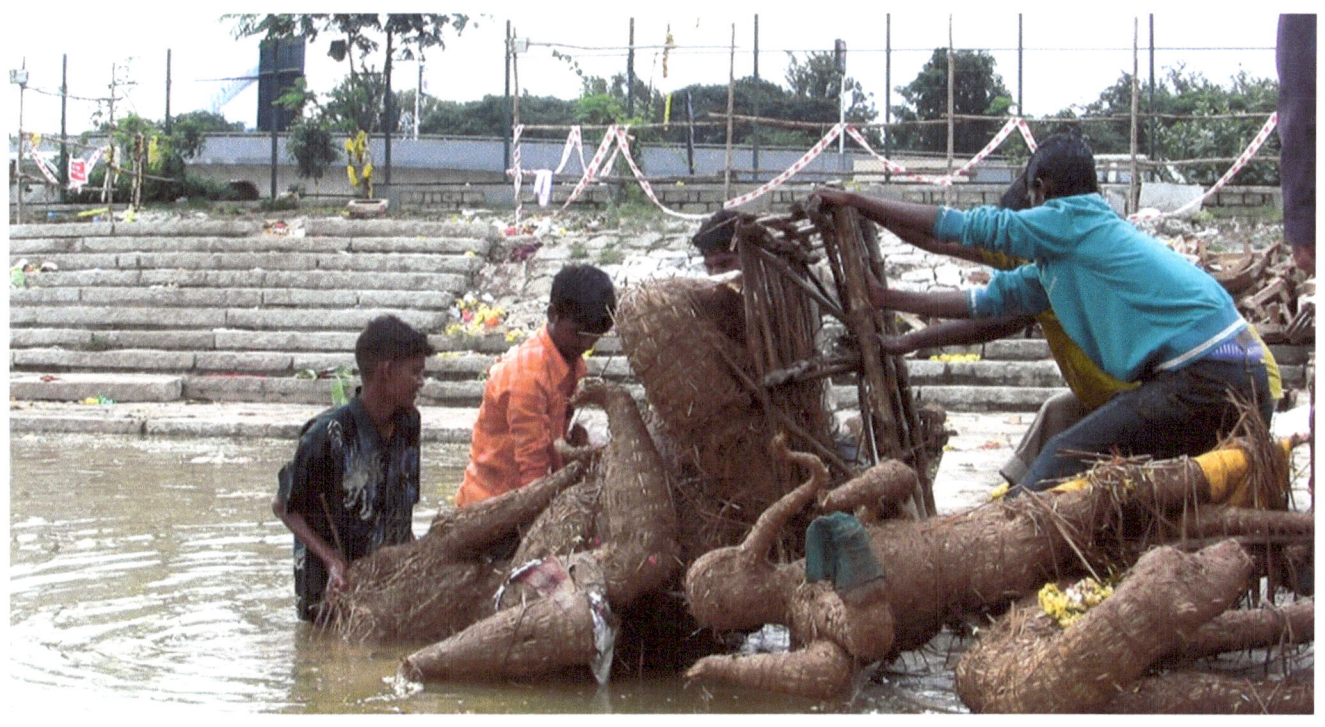

Smriti Mehra, still from *Tade*, 2010.

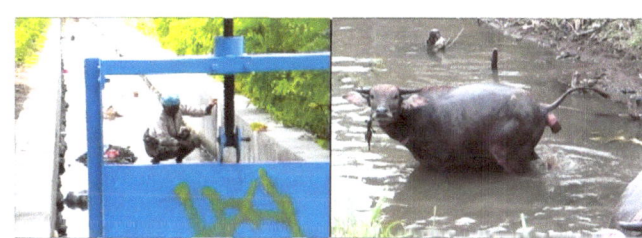

Monika Hapsari, stills from *Big Trash*, 2011.

Unsafe water is the biggest killer of children under five; around 90% of all diarrheal deaths are in this age group.

Manure from cows raised on factory farms ends up in waste lagoons, where it trickles into groundwater, streams, rivers.

One pound of beef requires 12,000 pounds of water, factoring in irrigation for feed crops, watering, transportation, storage, and other farm-to-market calculations.

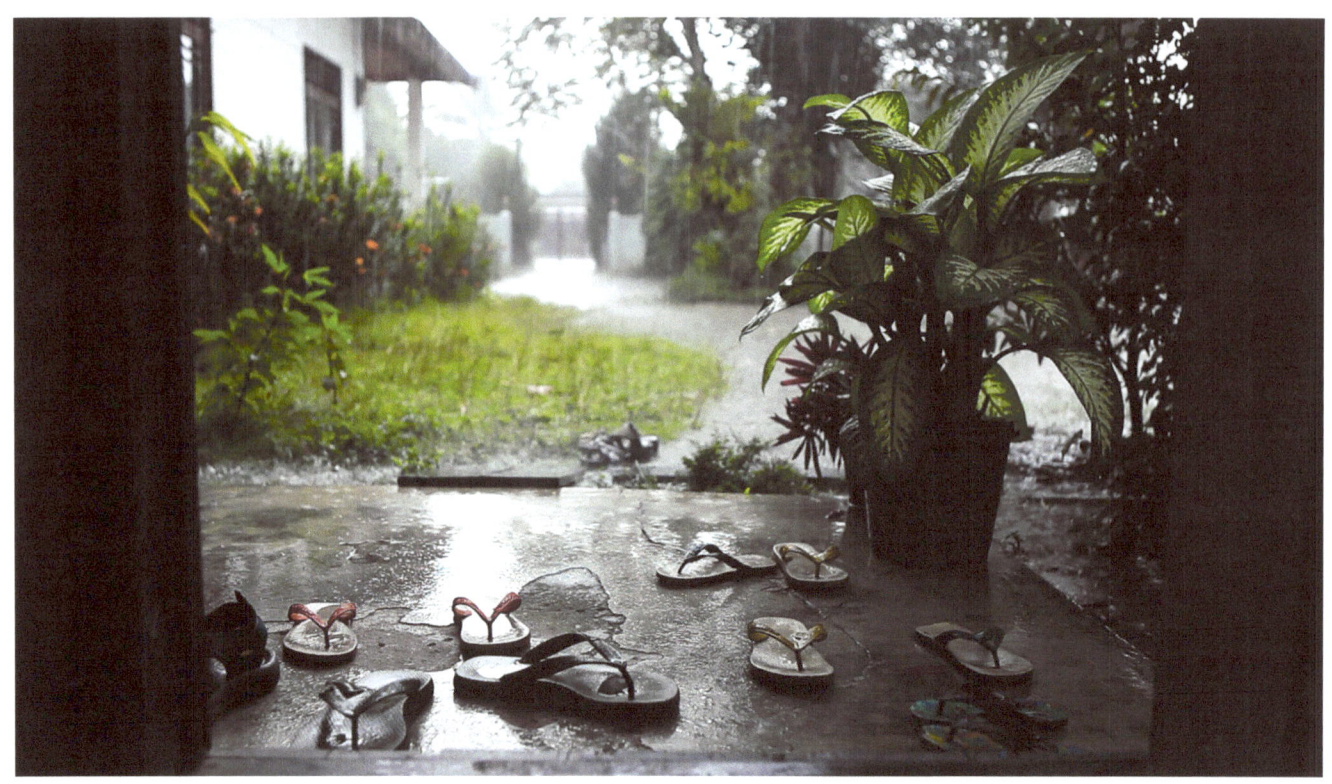

Jason Houston, still from *Indonesian Borneo: Rain Meditation*, 2009.

Tsunamis, also called seismic sea waves – or, incorrectly, tidal waves – generally are caused by earthquakes under the ocean floor.

Since the 1950s, worldwide, the average intensity of storms has increased, correlating with the increase of sea surface temperatures in the tropics.

As seawater reaches inland, it can cause destructive erosion, flooding of wetlands, contamination of aquifers and agricultural soils, and lost habitat for fish, birds, and plants.

Eighty percent of all illness in the developing world comes from water-borne diseases.

Leaders of countries experiencing the worst flooding are planning floating cities and/or considering moving their entire populations to neighboring countries.

The term "global water crisis" can imply only shortage. But there are many other deadly dimensions, too, as demonstrated by so-called Superstorm Sandy, which made landfall in New Jersey in 2012.

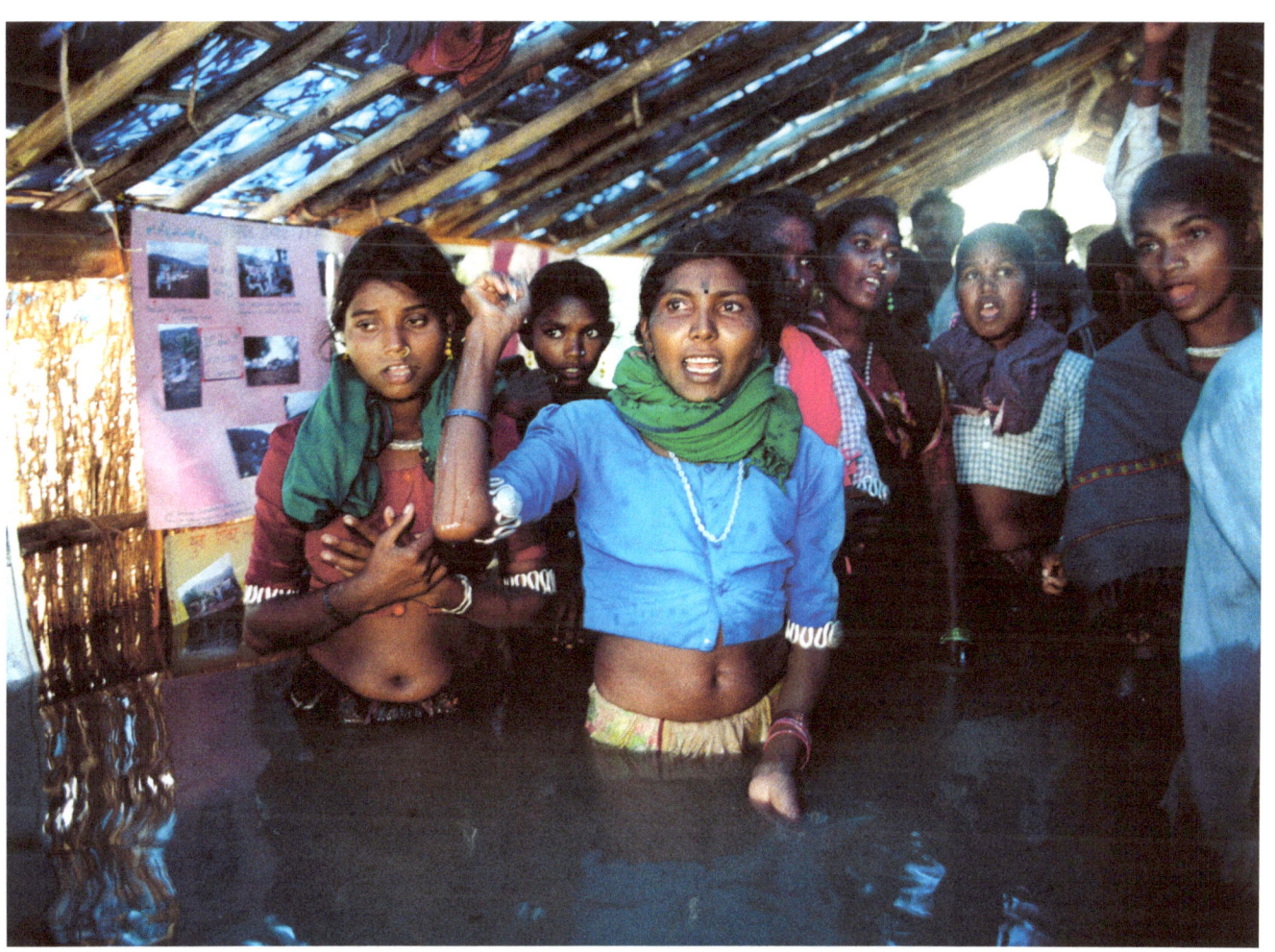

Carla Pataky and International Rivers, still from *A River Runs Through Us*, 2010.

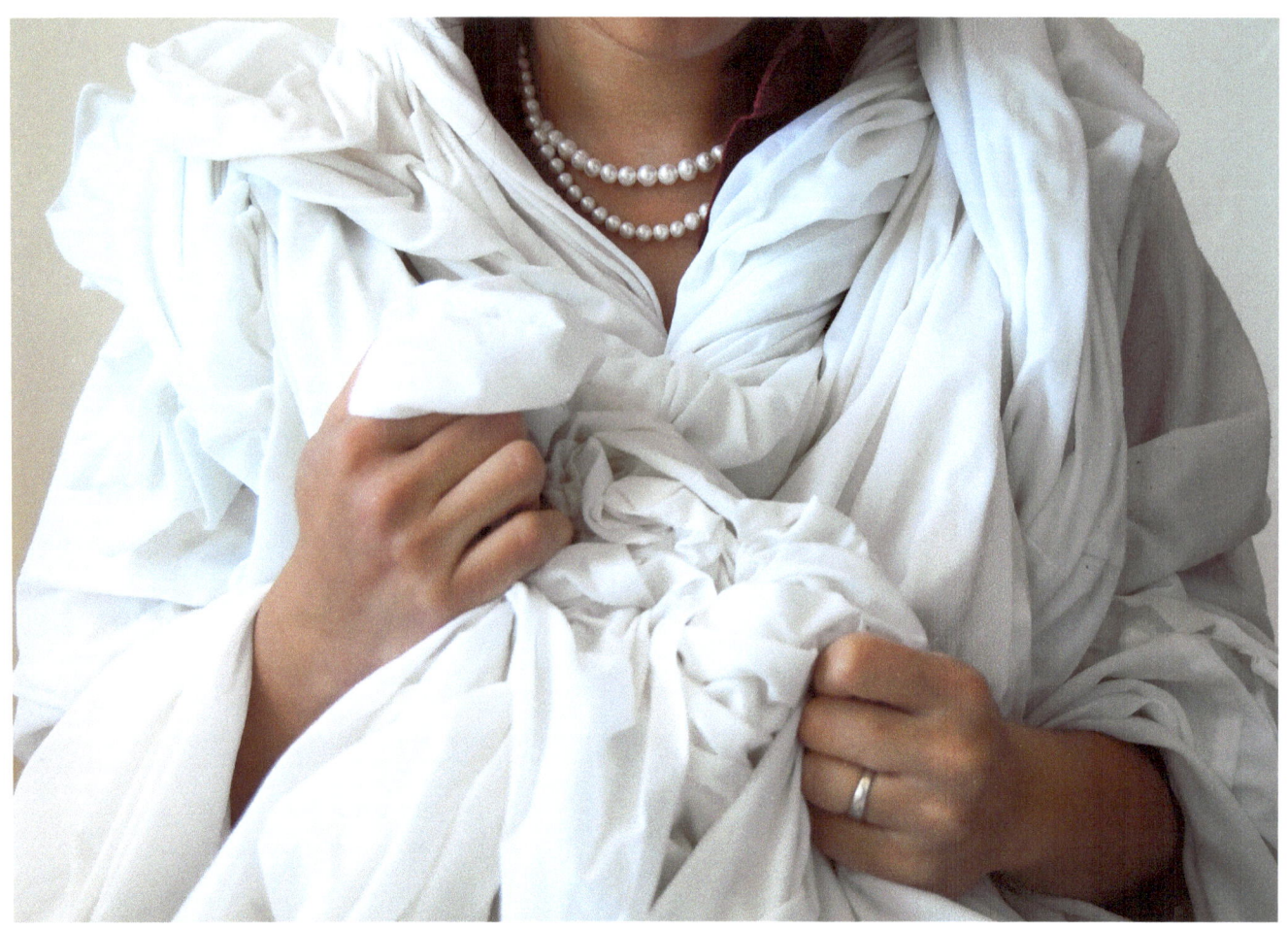

Gazelle Samizay, still from *This Will be the Last*, 2009.

"It is often too late by the time the government reacts."

– Vandana Shiva, philosopher, environmental activist, author, and eco feminist

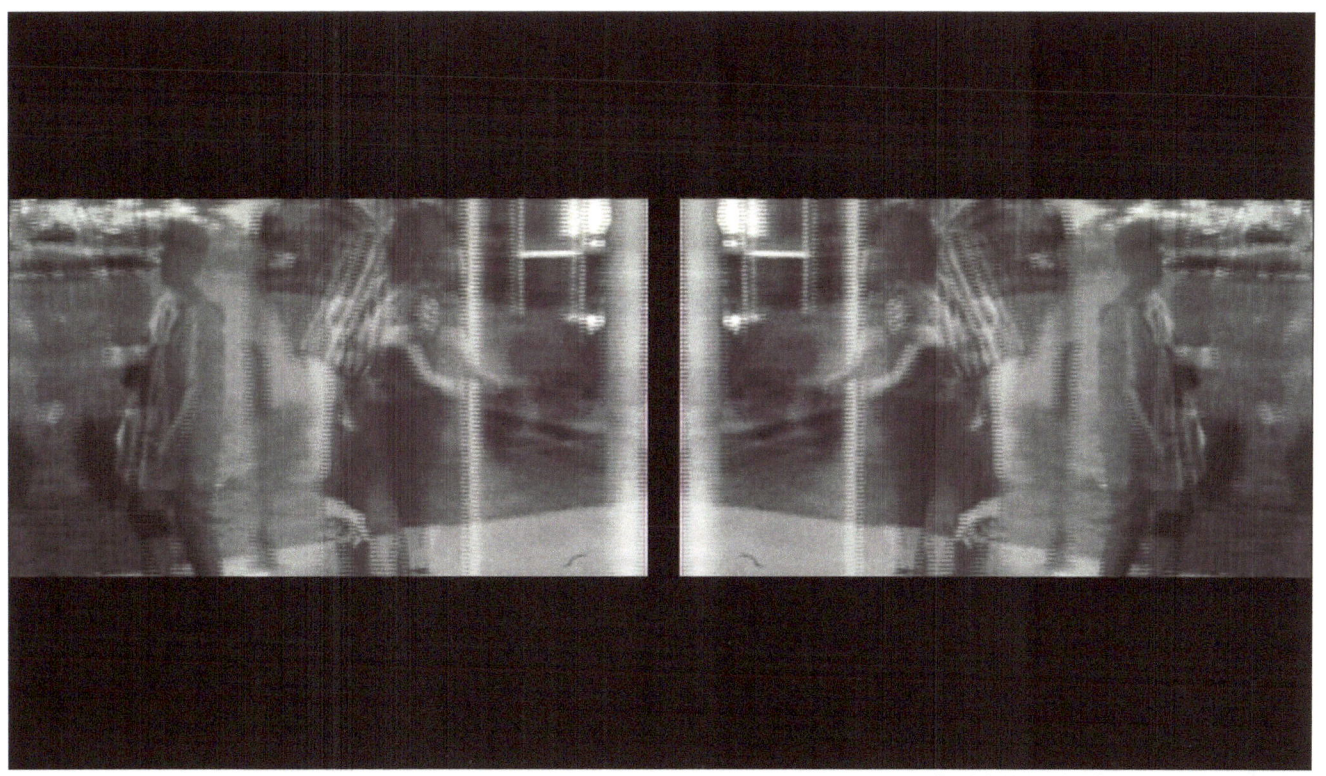

Patrizia Monzani, still from *found footage*, 2006.

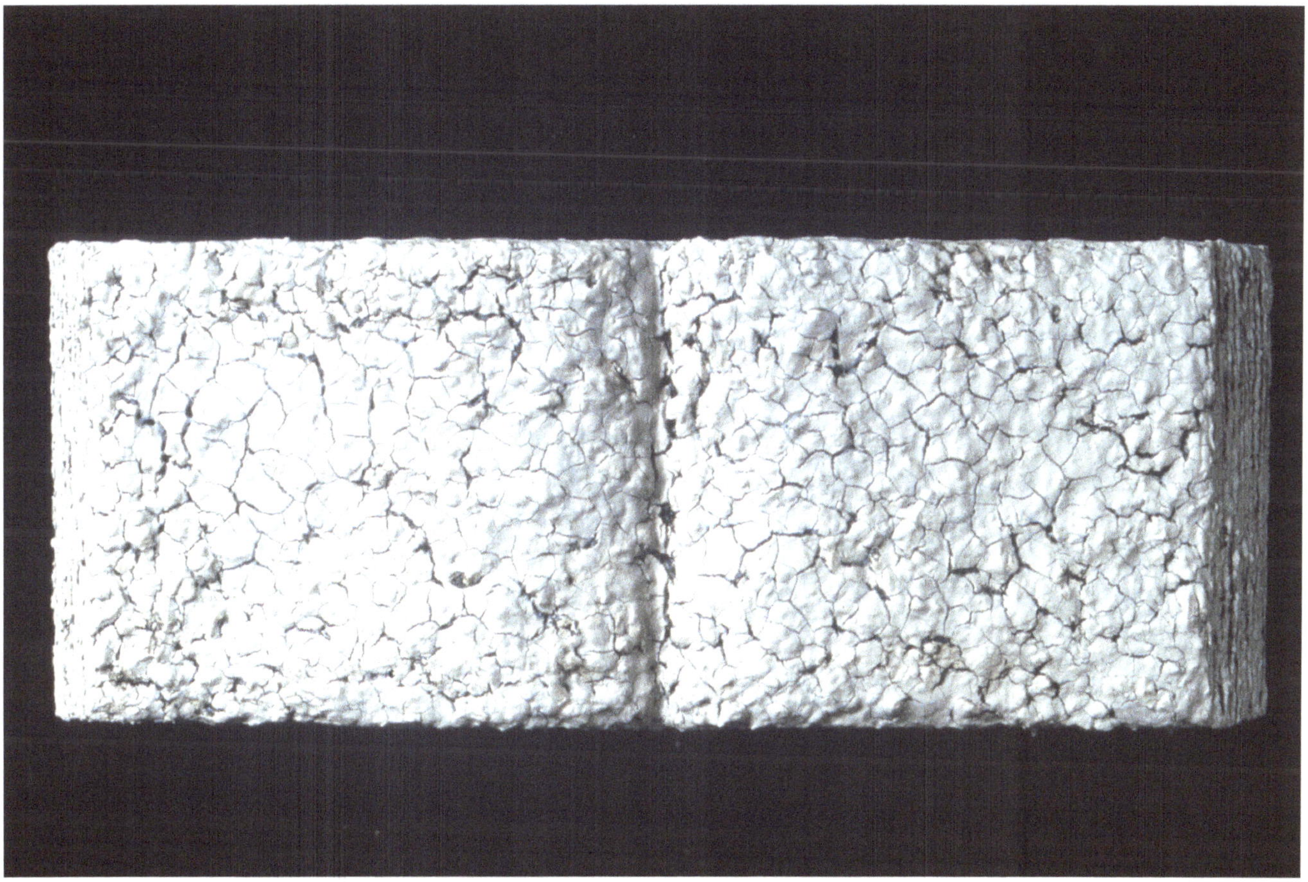

Basia Irland, still from *Book of Drought: A Water Memory*, 2009.

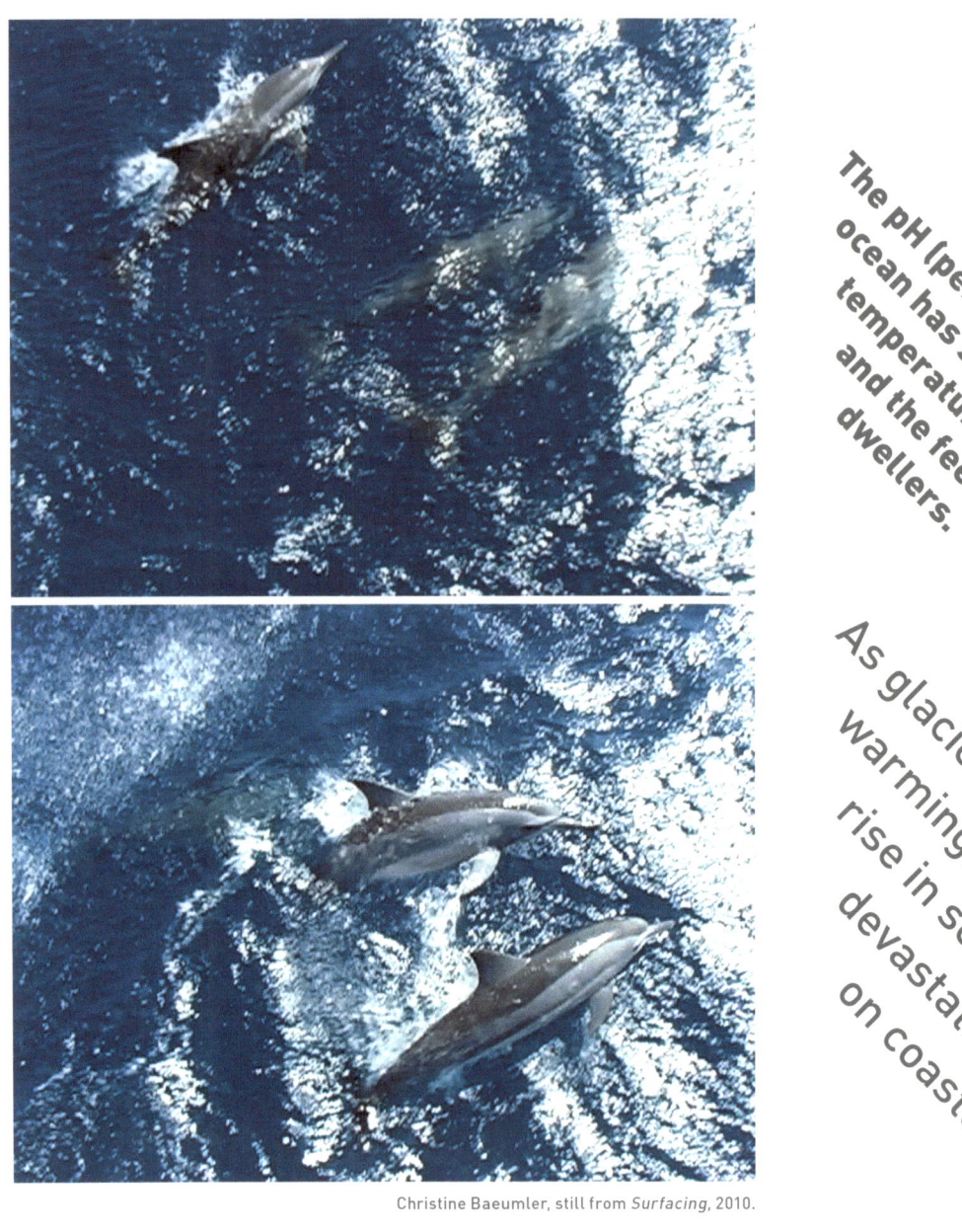

Christine Baeumler, still from *Surfacing*, 2010.

The pH (percentage hydrogen) of the ocean has shifted, changing water temperatures, current patterns, and the feeding patterns of ocean dwellers.

As glaciers melt due to global warming, even a small rise in sea levels can have devastating effects on coastal habitats.

Sources: United Nations Agencies (WHO, UNICEF, UNDP), World Water Development Report, Sierra Club, New York Times, AlterNet, water.org, matadornetwork.org, alternativeradio.org (Maude Barlow: "Peak Water" "The Global Water Crisis"), Water and Sanitation Program, NASA, National Geographic, Disasters, Disaster Preparedness Fact Sheet, Water Encyclopedia, Food and Water Watch, Dangers of Fracking.com, Greenpeace, Global Research.ca, National Public Radio, Vandana Shiva, Alex Prud'homme, Gasland, John Robbins.

The Artists

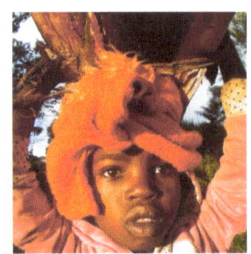

Evan Abramson & Carmen Elsa Lopez/USA
Carbon for Water

www.carbonforwaterfilm.com / www.facebook.com/carbonforwaterfilm

Evan Abramson and **Carmen Elsa Lopez** are filmmakers, photographers and new parents based in rural northwest Connecticut. Together they write, direct, shoot, edit, and produce. In 2010, they formed Cows in the Field, a production house focused on telling the stories of people whose lives are impacted by social and environmental crises around the globe — and on finding solutions. Their 2011 documentary *Carbon for Water* premiered at the Planet in Focus Environmental Film Festival in Toronto, winning Best International Short Film. It has gone on to win more than two dozen other awards, including the Sir Edmund Hillary Award for Environmental Film at the 2012 Mountain Film Awards; Best Short Documentary at the 2011 California International Shorts Fest; Best in Festival Documentary, Audience Choice Award and Social Entrepreneurship Outstanding Merit Award at the 2012 The MIX International Film Festival; Best Educational Film at the 2012 Mexico International Film Festival; Best Short Documentary at the 2012 Geneva Film Festival; and Highly Commended at the Development and Climate Days Film Festival at COP-17 in Durban, South Africa. Evan's 2010 documentary *When the Water Ends* won – among other awards – the Golden Drop First Prize at the International Water and Film Events at the 2012 World Water Forum, Prior to filmmaking, Carmen worked in journalism, marketing, and as an aid worker in post-earthquake Haiti. She studied film at NYU and the School of Visual Arts and holds a B.A. in political science from The Catholic University and a certificate in international studies from Johns Hopkins University. A self-taught filmmaker, Evan previously worked as a photojournalist. His images have been published widely, including in The Atlantic, National Geographic, The New York Times, The Washington Post, Guardian Weekend Magazine, FT Weekend, The Sunday Times and Courier Japan.

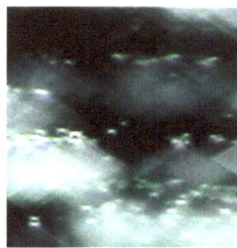

Diane Armitage/USA
The Great River

Diane Armitage is an artist in Santa Fe, New Mexico, working in digital video. She has a BFA in Ceramics and an MFA in Sculpture from the University of New Mexico. She studied Digital Media at the Santa Fe Community College, where she established the Art History program in 1999. She has taught Art Studio for the University of New Mexico and the History of Film for Santa Fe University of Art and Design. Her work in video and new media has been shown throughout the Southwest since 2000. She is featured in *100 Artists of the Southwest* (Schiffer Books, 2006).

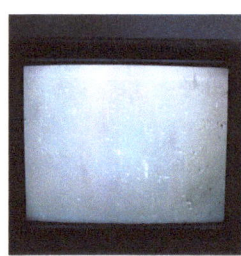

Ruben Aubrecht/Germany
april

www.rubenaubrecht.net

Ruben Aubrecht studied computer and video art at the Academy of Fine Arts in Vienna, Austria, from 2001 to 2006. He has participated in exhibitions throughout Europe, as well as in New York, Moscow, Mexico City, and Sydney, with residencies in Bilbao, Mexico City, and New York. In 2011 he received the advancement award from the Sezession Darmstadt in Germany. He lives and works in Berlin.

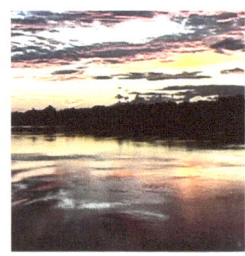

Christine Baeumler/USA
Amazon Twilight & Surfacing

www.christinebaeumler.net

Christine Baeumler is Associate Professor in the Department of Art at the University of Minnesota. She has a BA in Fine Arts from Yale University and an MFA from Indiana University. She is currently the Artist-in-Residence in the Capitol Region Watershed District. She maintains both a studio and community arts-based practice. The studio work includes painting, photography, and installation, based largely on travel to World Heritage sites, such as the Australian and Amazon rain forests, the Great Barrier Reef, and the Galapagos Islands. Her collaborative community-based environmental work involves the ecological restoration of urban green spaces with attention to increasing biodiversity, providing habitat, improving both the water quality and aesthetic dimension of the sites. She is a recipient of numerous prestigious grants and her artwork is in the collections of Ecolab, Ceridian Corporation, Mayo Clinic, the Walker Art Center, the Minneapolis Institute of Art, the Minnesota Historical Society, and the Minnesota University Foundation. She is currently a member of Mapping Spectral Traces, an international research center based in the UK that focuses on a site-specific practice.

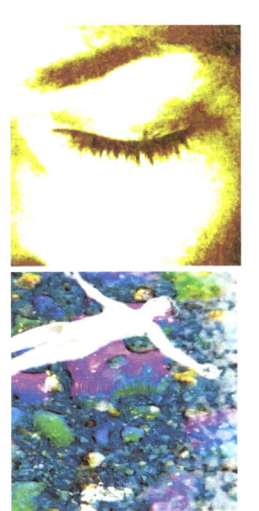

Krisanne Baker/USA

Upstream to Downstream (In Our Bloodstreams) & World Water Crises: Potential Effects/ Cumulative Effects

www.krisannebaker.com

Krisanne Baker is a global water activist and life-long lover of water. Her various works, whether paintings or sculptural installations, and her growing list of experimental/documentary short films all focus on concerns for water quality, availability, and water rights. The artist lives on the Medomak River estuary in Maine, where her observations of the water and her community further inspire her local work, as well as her short art documentary videos on both local and global water issues. Baker hopes to collaborate with scientists on water issues, putting the visuals in context with the facts. When not in the studio, Baker teaches environmental art and digital imaging at the University of Maine at Farmington.

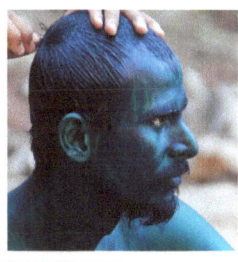

Manoj Baviskar/India

I Came... I Saw... Prayed for Someone Whom I Love

www.manojbaviskar.blogspot.in

Manoj Baviskar was born in Aurangabad and works in Baroda, India. He is currently a guest teacher in the Department of Fine Art at Tripura University in India and was a lecturer at K.K.Wagh College of Fine Art in Nashik, Maharashtra, India. He received his post-diploma in Fine Arts-Creative Sculpture from Manonmaniam Sundaranar University and has participated in numerous exhibitions. His time-based work takes shape from his immediate surroundings, reflecting the cultural and social aspects of that environment, and often displaying the process. His choices of materials depend on availability, differing according to place and situation. In recent years, he has been performing, using his body and voice in spaces, as well as on video, in photographs and installations. His performances are atmospheric, sometimes ritualistic, showing the cyclical circles of destruction and renewal, as well as formal and conceptual ideas and the framework of personal references that inform the fragile divide between his life and his art. He has been awarded the 2011 UNESCO/Aschberg Brusaries for Visual Artists residency at California's Djerassi Resident Artists Program and had major performances at the Theertha International Artist Residency in Colombo, Sri Lanka, the Shatana International Site Specific Workshop in Shatana, Jordan, and the International Site Specific Workshop organized by Pariwartan, Gowahati, India.

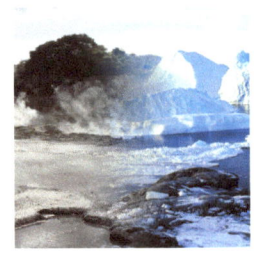

Åsa Maria Bengtsson & Ewa Cederstam/Sweden
FLOW

www.asamariabengtsson.se /
www.mantarayfilm.se

Åsa Maria Bengtsson is a visual artist from Malmö, Sweden, where she was educated at the Forum School of Graphics. She works in various techniques: sculpture, photography, drawing, installations, public works, film, and video. She has produced numerous short films and video installations and has received several grants and awards. In 1996, she received a ten-year working grant from the Swedish Arts Grants Committee. Her interest lies in nature, the environment, and human identity. In 2011, she completed the short film *Fermentity*.

Ewa Cederstam was born in Malmö, Sweden, educated as a still photographer at Malmö Yrkesskola and as a cinematographer at Stockholm Academy of Dramatic Arts. She holds an MA in filmmaking and directing at The School of Film Directing in Gothenburg. She has been a cinematographer on a great number of documentaries, as well as fiction films, and she has co-directed three films. Her first full-length documentary, *Dare Remember*, premiered in 2012.

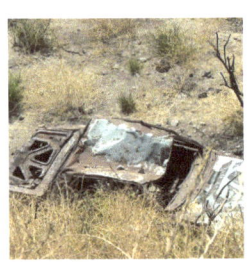

Beth Block/USA
Leaky Mountain

www.gidgetal-digital.com

Beth Block is a filmmaker and media artist who has worked in 16mm film, still photography, and installation. She received her BFA in art from Kent State University and her MFA in film from the California Institute for the Arts. Her 16mm experimental and documentary films have shown internationally and are included in the collections of the Library of Congress, Projections on Lake, and the Canadian Film Board. They have screened at MoMA, won awards at the Ann Arbor Film Festival, and toured at the Sinking Creek, Black Maria and Philadelphia film festivals. She has worked in 1080p digital cinema since 2007. Her film 57 Jobless premiered at the 2010 Athens Film Festival, where Leaky Mountain also premiered in 2011. She has worked professionally in the film industry throughout her career, first doing optical effects for films including *Terminator 2*, *Altered States*, and *Wolfen*, and more recently as a digital compositing artist creating visual effects for motion pictures including *Astronaut Farmer*, *Looney Tunes: Back in Action*, *The Sponge Bob Square Pants Movie*, and *James and the Giant Peach*. She has served on the board of Los Angeles Filmforum, including three terms as president, and is a founding member and current president of the NewTown Pasadena Foundation. She currently teaches film production in the School of Cinematic Studies at the University of Southern California and is a freelance cinematographer and visual effects artist.

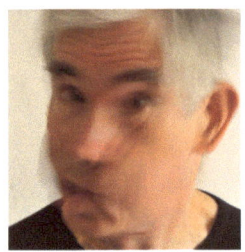

Jaap Blonk/Netherlands
Flababble 1

Image and Sound: Jaap Blonk
(www.jaapblonk.com)

Camera: Lisette Stalenhoef
(lisettestalenhoef.com)

Jaap Blonk was born in 1953 in Woerden, Holland, and is a self-taught composer, performer, and poet. He studied mathematics at university, but in the late 1970s took up the saxophone and started to compose music. A few years later, he discovered his potential as a vocal performer, at first in reciting poetry and later with improvisations and his own compositions. For almost two decades, the voice was his main medium for the discovery and development of new sounds. Around 2000, he started work with electronics, at first using samples of his own voice, then extending the field to include pure sound synthesis. In 2006, he took a year off from performing and renewed his interest in mathematics, researching the possibilities of algorithmic composition for the creation of music, visual animation, and poetry. As a vocalist, he is unique for his powerful stage presence and almost childlike freedom in improvisation, combined with a keen grasp of structure. He has performed on all continents of the world except Antarctica. With the use of live electronics and visuals, the scope and range of his concerts have extended considerably. He has collaborated with many musicians and ensembles in the field of contemporary and improvised music.

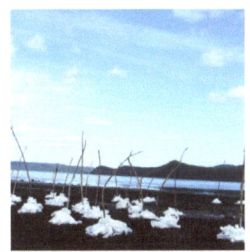

Claudia Borgna/Italy/UK/USA
Sweep & Weep, Weep & Sweep & Poise of Tides

claudiaborgna.com

Claudia Borgna was born in Hamburg, Germany, and reared in Italy. After graduating from Genoa University in foreign literature, she moved to London. In 2005, she received a degree in Fine Art at the London Metropolitan University. She lived and exhibited her work in London for fifteen years, then began leading a nomadic life pursuing her art all over the world, with shows in Berlin, Europe, Mexico, and the United States. She has attended fellowship residencies in the US, Canada, and Europe, is the recipient of both the Joan Mitchell and the Jackson Pollock and Lee Krasner grants and was awarded the Royal British Society of Sculptors Bursary Award, the Pritzker Foundation Endowed Fellowship Award, and in 2010 she was voted The Public Speaks Winner for the Broomhill (UK) National Sculpture Prize (UK). Her work investigates what she calls the "evolution of landscape," a process started and effected by modern lifestyles and consumerism. Her installations are the materialization of an ongoing observation and questioning of how the "plastic" and natural realms interact and thereby create new ephemeral orders. She mainly works with recycled plastic bags, which travel with her wherever she goes. She is currently attending the Public Practice MFA program at OTIS College of Art and Design in Los Angeles.

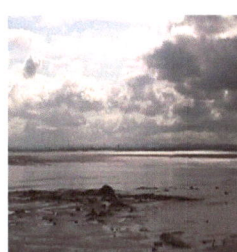

James Brady/UK
Floodland Study #1

www.james-brady.blogspot.com

www.jamesbrady.jux.com

James Brady is an interdisciplinary artist, curator and activist based in North West England. Through his diverse practice he endeavors to reveal creative patterns and dynamics embodied within our symbiosis with places, environments, and natural systems. At heart, Brady is a romantic and finds joy in exploring the sublime and poetics of nature. His imagination is captured by the deep-time aesthetics of landscape ecologies. In creatively exploring this fascination, his recent artworks have incorporated digital video, field recordings, texts, performance, and organic matter. Brady's activity as a curator is rooted in interdisciplinary collaboration and experimentation, driven by a desire to connect people, ideas, and actions in order to create complex and resonant relationships that might otherwise remain unrealized. He regards this socially engaged practice (a kind of social sculpture) as facilitating the emergence of "ecological consciousness." He is the Associate Curator at Ultimate Holding Company (UHC), Manchester, UK; an Associate of the CIWEM Arts & Environment Network, UK; and an Associate of the International Eco Art Network. In 2013 he became an affiliate of Cape Farewell.

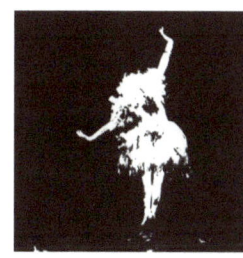

Fiammetta De Michele/Italy
Louisiana

fiammettademichele.com

Fiammetta De Michele was born in Milan in 1984 and received her degree in Visual Arts from the Accademia di Belle Arti di Brera in 2009. In her work, she touches all fields of aesthetic experience, as a sole sensory fabric without medial distinction. Her artworks recall surreal environments in which the essence of the elements hides in the skin of the quotidian, ready to be revealed. Her photographs, videos, installations, and performances consider the contemporary age and in her vision, the female image becomes a modern spiritual model. Her work has been exhibited at, among others, Pinacoteca di Follonica, Teatro delle Rocce in Gavorrano, Castel'Azzara, Sorano and Porto Santo Stefano, Lucca Centre of Contemporary Art, Samson Gallery, Boston, and the Triennale di Milano. She is represented by Milan's Avantgarden Gallery.

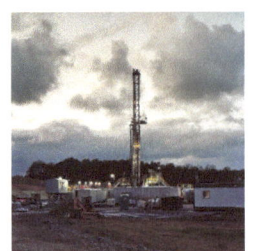

Jacques del Conte/USA
A Colossal Fracking Mess

boxerbabeprod.com

Jacques del Conte is a New York City-based documentary filmmaker. He is often commissioned by Vanity Fair Magazine for online video stories ranging in subject matter from the earthquake in Haiti to the Sundance Film Festival to hydraulic fracturing in the Northeast to profiles of artists and writers. He began his career in still photography, studying under renowned artists such as Larry Fink, Stephen Shore, and Vik Muniz at Bard College. He co-owns – with his partner Chandra Ratner – a video production company, boxerbabe llc, directing and editing short- and long-form documentary, music video, and advertising.

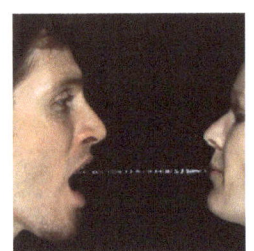

Robert Ladislas Derr/USA
Conservation of Momentum

home1.arts.ohio-state.edu/derr34

Robert Ladislas Derr uses various modes of making, which center on a barrage of questions about life and art. He translates the world around him through visual manifestations that leave viewers with a sideways glance. For Derr, life is a performance—it sets the stage for his making. Exhibitions and performances of his work include the Mendel Art Gallery, Schirn Kunsthalle, Wexner Center for the Arts, and Irish Film Institute, to name a few. Among his awards are the Urbana Public Arts Commission, Lower Manhattan Cultural Council, and Ohio Arts Council. Some of the collections holding his work include Loyola University Museum of Art, Miami-Dade Public Library, and Indiana University Art Museum. Derr received his MFA from the Rhode Island School of Design and BFA from the Art Academy of Cincinnati.

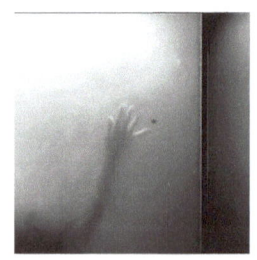

Mary Rachel Fanning/USA
The Trophy

maryrachelfanning.com

Mary Rachel Fanning is an artist who currently lives and works in Chicago. She has exhibited nationally and internationally and worked with non-profits and institutions such as Street-Level Youth Media, the Museum of Contemporary Photography, the International Center of Bethlehem, and Al-Feneiq Cultural Centre. She is a co-founder of 6+: a women's art collective. Her influences and motivations are derived from her upbringing. "Raised by a pair of progressive educators in the Deep South," she says, "I am fascinated with people's stories, both public and private. Often my cultural interactions encounter the sharp edges of economics, race, age, social friction, and the American Dream. However, what remains most important to me is how my subjects (who I see as collaborators) communicate their relationship with the places they live, with others, and even myself, the artist."

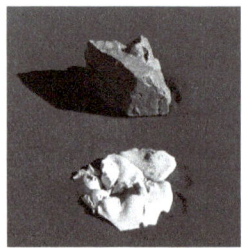

Diego Fiori/Austria & Italy
Silenzio: Birth and Death of the Alter Ego

Edited and directed with Olga Pohankova

Diego Fiori was born in Rome and lives and works in Rome and Vienna. After receiving his degree at the Academy of Fine Arts in Rome, he began following the ideas of Giorgio Agamben at the University of IUAV of Venice and attended the courses of Giovanni Reale at the State University of Milan. In recent years, after various artistic experiences relative to "declinations" of the sculpture, Fiori has been developing a particular form of video art and, like a shaman, evokes solemn sensations of ancestry in his videos. Silenzio won 2nd prize at the IN OUT 2010 Film Festival, Laznia Center of Contemporary Art in Poland.

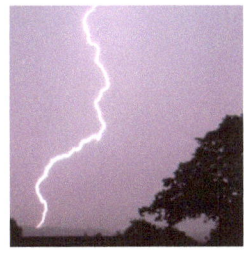

Georgie Friedman/USA
Light of the Storm

www.georgiefriedman.com

Georgie Friedman is an award-winning American artist currently based in Boston, Massachusetts. She received her MFA from the School of the Museum of Fine Arts, Boston, in conjunction with Tufts University, and her BA from the University of California, Santa Cruz. She has exhibited throughout the United States. She currently teaches at Boston College and Massachusetts College of Art. In 2010, The Boston Phoenix called her "one of the most exciting new-media artists in the region." Friedman's videos, photographs, and video-installations consider the psychological and physical relationships of individuals to various uncontrollable natural forces. She reframes our typical viewing relationships to the sky, water or light, so that perception and experience become primary elements of the work. Although each piece has its own specific theme and emphasis, she creates new experiential spaces for viewers to inhabit, highlighting our tenuous interconnections to the various elements and our relationships to built, digital, and natural environments.

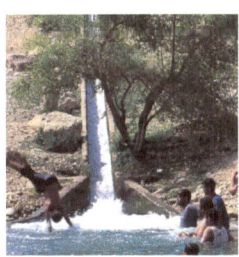
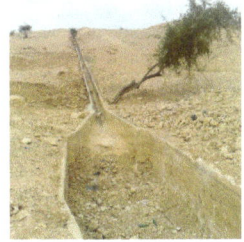

Friends of the Earth Middle East/Palestine/Jordan/Israel
Good Water Neighbors

www.foeme.org

Friends of the Earth Middle East (FoEME) is a unique organization that brings together Jordanian, Palestinian, and Israeli environmentalists and whose primary objective is the promotion of cooperative efforts to protect our shared environmental heritage. In so doing, FoEME seeks to advance both sustainable regional development and the creation of necessary conditions for lasting peace in our region. FoEME has offices in Amman, Bethlehem, and Tel-Aviv and is a member of Friends of the Earth International, the largest grassroots environmental organization in the world. FoEME is a project-oriented NGO, using a "top-down" (advocacy) approach coupled with a "bottom-up" (grass roots / community) strategy that has proven to be a very effective work model. FoEME has received numerous honors, including the Skoll Award in 2009, the 2010 Green Globe Award for best environmental education project, and the 2011 Outstanding Leadership Award from the International Development Committee of the Association for Conflict Resolution. In 2013 FoEME was named one of the top 100 NGOs in the world by the Global Journal.

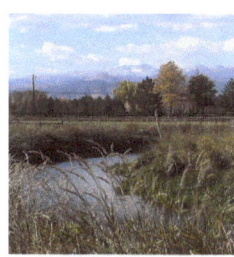
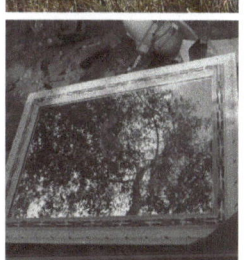

J. Gluckstern/USA
Ditches of Boulder & lyons, co, 10-10-13

J. Gluckstern's films and film-related works have been shown in Korea, Mexico, and throughout the United States. He's received numerous grants, awards, and commissions, among them a professional development fellowship from the Robert Flaherty Film Seminar in 2006, and he's taught film production at the University of Colorado-Boulder since 1999. He's also been an arts journalist since the late 1980s, writing about film and art for many regional and national publications, and received his MFA in media from the University of Colorado at Boulder in 2007.

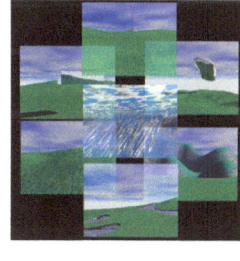

Henry Gwiazda/USA
there's whispering

www.henrygwiazda.com

Henry Gwiazda is a new media artist/composer whose artistic trajectory has taken him from sampling, sound effects, and immersive technologies to his current work with new media. This comprehensive artistic approach has resulted in work that is multimedia in nature and focused on movement. Gwiazda's works are regularly screened in festivals and galleries throughout the world including New York, Paris, Madrid, Cairo, Amsterdam, Beijing, Berlin, Sao Paolo, Naples, Marseilles, Seoul, Damascus, Athens, Istanbul, Moscow, and many others. He won First Prize at Abstracta Cinema (Rome), Magmart Video Festival (Naples), Festival InOut (Gdansk), Second Prize at the Crosstalk Video Art Festival (Budapest), Third Prize at the GIGUK Video Art Festival (Giessen, Germany), and the Grand Prize for Best Audio at the 2008 DIGit Media Exposition (Narrowsburg, New York). His work is available on Innova Recordings.

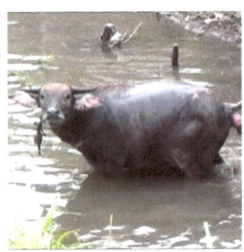

Monika Hapsari (Hapsari Dyah Aryani)/ Indonesia

Big Trash

Monika Hapsari (Hapsari Dyah Aryani) was born in Manokwari, Indonesia, and lives in Bantul Yogyakarta. She began her career as a graphics designer and art director for TV Borobudur Semarang in 2002. She has been a program director and news editor covering the 2004 tsunami in Aceh, the 2006 Yogyakarta earthquake, the eruption of Mount Merapi in 2006 and 2010, and the terrorist attack in Temanggung. In 2011, she was the resident artist for the Tropical Lab at Lassale University in Singapore. Her video art, *Lava Dance Merapi*, was displayed at the Taman Budaya Yogyakarta at ArtJog 2011, *Holopis Kuntul Baris* was shown at the May 2011 Indonesian Nite Video in Berlin, and *Tempeh Face*, was displayed at ICAS in September 2011.

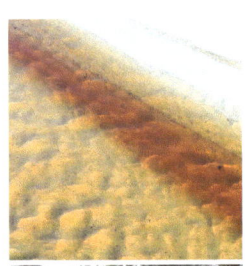
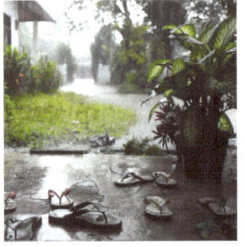

Jason Houston/USA

Indonesian Borneo: Water Meditation & Rain Meditation

jasonhouston.com

Jason Houston has worked in visual communication for more than 20 years, much of the time as an independent photographer / filmmaker addressing social and environmental issues. His images have been exhibited in museums, galleries, and public spaces across the country, and used by editorial and NGO clients worldwide to inform and inspire audiences to consider things that matter. He is a fellow of the International League of Conservation Photographers.

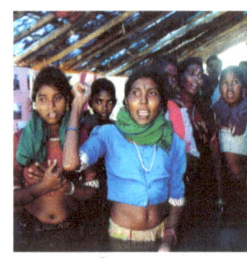

Carla Pataky & International Rivers/USA

A River Runs Through Us

www.internationalrivers.org

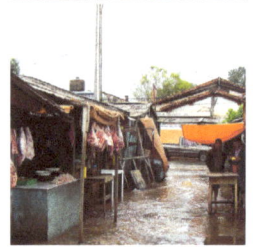

Carla Pataky is an independent filmmaker living in Mexico City, where she has been an active associate of Ecocomunidad, a non-profit organization, since 2008, and in addition has worked for more than six years with the indigenous community, Xi'ui, in the Sierra Gorda in the state of Querétaro, in a project involving kids in art. From 2007 through 2009, she coordinated an environmental education program on the coast of Oaxaca, teaching art and environment workshops with elementary school teachers and promoters in rural communities and organized a participatory video project with four communities in Oaxaca, dealing with solid wastes and community development. From 2002 to 2005, she coordinated "bulbo.tv," a program broadcast nationwide by Canal22 of short documentaries on the Tijuana-San Diego border and photographed the documentary *Once Upon a Time*, about violence against women in Mexico. She continues to be involved in various community development projects, working independently or in collaboration with other organizations such as Esperanza de México, Selva Negra, International Rivers, and Promotora de las Bellas Artes. Pataky has a BA in Visual Arts from the University of California, San Diego.

International Rivers has, since 1985, been at the heart of the global struggle to protect rivers and the rights of communities that depend on them, working with an international network of dam-affected people, grassroots organizations, environmentalists, human rights advocates, and others committed to stopping destructive river projects and promoting better options. International Rivers seeks a world where healthy rivers and the rights of local communities are valued and protected, where water and energy needs are met without degrading nature or increasing poverty, and where people have the right to participate in decisions that affect their lives. Based in five continents, International Rivers' staff has expertise in dams, energy, and water policy, climate change, and international financial institutions and supports partner organizations and dam-affected people by providing advice, training and technical assistance, and advocating on their behalf with governments, banks, companies, and international agencies. The work is focused in Latin America, Asia and Africa.

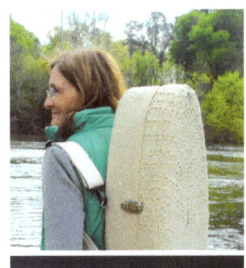

Basia Irland/USA
A Gathering of Waters: Rio Grande Source to Sea & Book of Drought: A Water Memory

www.basiairland.com

Basia Irland is an author, poet, sculptor, installation artist, and activist who creates international water projects, many of which are featured in her book, *Water Library* (University of New Mexico Press, 2007). The book focuses on projects the artist has created across three decades in Africa, Canada, Europe, South America, Southeast Asia, and the United States. Through her work, Irland offers a creative understanding of water while examining how communities of people, plants, and animals rely on this vital element. Irland is Professor Emerita, Department of Art and Art History, University of New Mexico, where she established the Arts and Ecology Program. She often works with scholars from diverse disciplines building rainwater harvesting systems; connecting communities and fostering dialogue along the entire length of rivers; filming and producing water documentaries; and creating waterborne disease projects around the world, most recently in Egypt, Ethiopia, India, and Nepal. She is regularly commissioned for river restoration projects, including in West Virginia on Decker's Creek, heavily polluted with acid mine drainage, and Georgia's Oconee River, with an emphasis on fresh-water diatoms. She worked via Internet with environmental artists on the Karun River, Shoushtar, Iran. Irland lectures and exhibits extensively and was the only artist (and the only woman) invited to participate in the 2010 Foundation for the Future's International World Water Crisis Forum in Seattle, Washington. She has received more than forty grants, including a Senior Fulbright Research Award for Southeast Asia, Woodrow Wilson Foundation Fellowship Grant and a National Oceanic and Atmospheric Research Grant. Her work is in collections and featured in books worldwide.

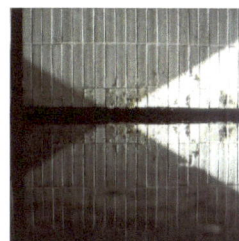

Robin Johnston/Scotland
Death of Light in Symmetry

cloudplasma.co.uk/lanvacette

Robin Johnston comes from a background that encouraged him to take an interest in the creative arts. Both his parents are retired art teachers, and are still practicing artists. Through their influence, Johnston developed and pursued an education in photography and video at James Watt College and Napier University in Scotland. During his studies, he produced a number of short film and video projects and improved his knowledge of photography and the history of the visual arts. During his time at Napier he began working as a freelance runner, PA, and technician with a number of small video-production companies in and around Edinburgh and Glasgow.

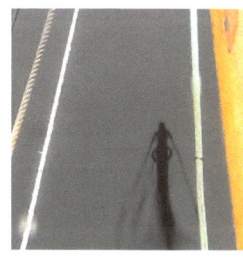

Pat Law/Scotland
Voyage

www.studiolog.heriot-toun.co.uk

Pat Law is a visual artist working across art forms and often in collaboration with artists of different disciplines. Her work is prompted by observation of the landscape encountered through voyages or travel. Having studied both art and ecological sciences, she has a strong interest in the natural environment, especially in northern latitudes. She was selected for an Arctic Circle expedition in 2012, sailing on a Tall Ship in the company of other artists and scientists around the coastline of Svalbard. She lives in the Scottish Borders where she also runs Heriot Toun Studio, a residential space for artists of all disciplines.

Shireen Malik/USA
Photographer

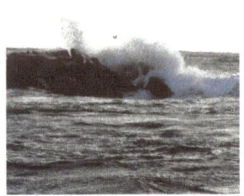

Shireen Malik has been a picture taker for as long as she can remember. People, places, things. The keeper of memories. Gradually, the passion for dedicated photography worked its way into her being. Photographing the natural world, the realm of infinite variety and constant change - sublime, powerful, beautiful, bizarre. Malik lived in south Florida for two years, photographing at the seashore most every day - capturing the many different moods of the ocean and the abundant life in and around the water's edge. Walking or jogging, toting a camera or two, stopping for moments or hours, taking hundreds of photos for the occasional aha! shot and those surprises along the way. Her photos for *Water, Water Everywhere* come from that Florida sojourn.

Liz Marshall/Canada
excerpt from Water on the Table

www.lizmars.com

Liz Marshall is a multi-award winning auteur filmmaker who fuses character-driven cinematic storytelling with social and environmental justice issues. Since the 1990s she has created a body of eleven documentary projects shot all over the world that focus on a range of subjects including: animal rights; the right to water movement; HIV/AIDS in sub-Saharan Africa; sweatshop labor; corporate-globalization; gender; censorship affecting writers and journalists and war-affected children. *Water On The Table* (2010) – which describes Maude Barlow's crusade to have water declared a human right and protected from privatization – is a Gemini-nominated theatrical and broadcast documentary and won the Best Canadian Feature Film Award at the 11th Annual Planet in Focus Environmental Film Festival. *The Ghosts in Our Machine,* explores the moral significance of animals and shines new light on the subject of animal rights, within the context of our voracious consumer-driven world.

Smriti Mehra/India
Tade

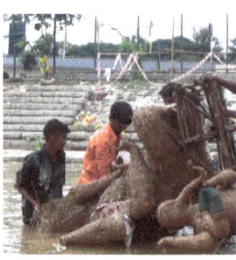

Smriti Mehra is a video artist who lives and works in Bangalore, India. She has earned her MFA in Media Art from the Nova Scotia College of Art and Design in Halifax, Canada with a scholarship from the American Association of University Women Educational Foundation. She is currently an artist-in-residence at Bangalore's Centre for Experimental Media Art and she also teaches at the Srishti School of Art, Design and Technology, where she studied as an undergraduate. Her video works have played at many festivals, including Voices from the Waters –the third international film festival on water in Bangalore –The Images Festival, Monitor 7 and Monitor 3 in Toronto, Denmark's Made in Video Festival, Photophobia 8 in Hamilton, Canada, and Images De l Inde at the Centre Pompidou in France. *Tade* was produced in collaboration with research assistant, Tahireh Lal.

Patrizia Monzani/Italy
found footage

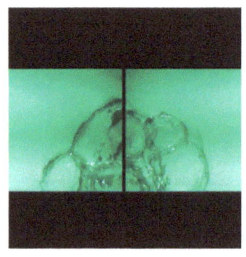

www.patriziamonzani.tk

Patrizia Monzani works as a videomaker, curator, and editor in Italy. Her fields of interest are documentaries, animation, and video art. She has authored several videopoems in collaboration with contemporary poets. Her latest work is the documentary film *The Science of Panic*, thus far screened in Italy, Spain, and South America.

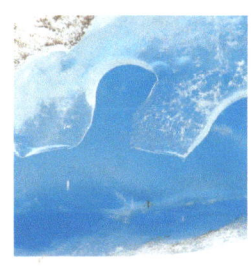

Jessica Plumb/USA
Climate Change: An Intimate Portrait
www.plumbproductions.com

Jessica Plumb is a filmmaker and video artist who believes in the power of story. Her work ranges from site-specific video and sound installations to directing and producing documentary films. The underlying theme running through her films is the relationship between people and place. Her favorite tools are light, rhythm, words, and movement. She has screened video installation pieces at galleries throughout the Pacific Northwest, and worked on films screened at festivals in numerous capacities, behind the camera and in post-production. She holds a BA from Yale University and an MFA in interdisciplinary arts from Goddard College. She has pursued continuing education in film production at 911 Media in Seattle, Anderson Ranch, and the New School University in New York. Currently, she is producing and editing a feature-length documentary on the removal of the Elwha River dams and the power of people who love a place.
She is the founder of Plumb Productions, which creates multi-media stories for non-profit organizations, individual artists and other clients.

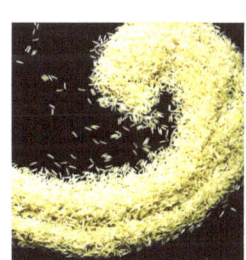

Carolyn Radlo and Alanna Simone/USA
Rice Relief
thecarolynandalannashow.com

Carolyn Radlo and **Alanna Simone** are artists based in California, who comprise C+A Projects. They collaborate on projects dealing with social and political situations communicated through sparse text and evocative imagery. They like to work with words, images, and meaning without necessarily relying on narrative or linearity. Many of their projects begin with a shared history or attitude, but then explore the differences and similarities that show up in work made side by side; they are always guided and supported by chance. Radlo's formal education was in English and Religious Studies at the University of California, Santa Barbara, and Simone has a degree in Film and Video Production from Brooks Institute of Photography. Their life-long, multi-faceted collaboration has, in recent years, evolved from mother-daughter to artist-artist.

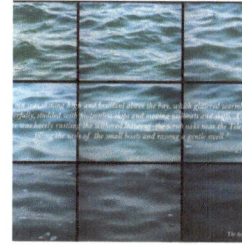

Tobias Rosenberger/Germany
Sevastopol in August
www.tobiasrosenberger.de

Tobias Rosenberger studied Applied Theatre Studies in Giessen, Germany, and works at the crossroads of theatre, new media art, and installation. Besides various performances (Festival Junger Talente, Frankfurter Positionen, Körber Studio Junge Regie) he has realized installations for the German and French embassies in Sana'a, Yemen, the Goethe Institut in Barcelona, and Franken Architekten. He was a three-time participant of Luminale Frankfurt (2006, 2008, 2010) and has exhibited widely, including Lyon, France, Macau, Copenhagen, Denmark, Liverpool, England, Katowice, Poland, Mexico City, Osnabrück, Germany, Beijing, and Esslingen/Neckar, Germany. Rosenberger has been awarded numerous grants and held residencies in Europe, India, and Asia.

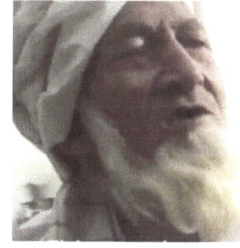

Alka Sadat/Afghanistan
The Kabul Sea
www.royafilmhouse.org

Alka Sadat was born in Herat, Afghanistan. With her sister, Roya Sadat, she founded the Roya Film House production company and is a coordinator of the Afghanistan International Women's Film Festival. Her own moving documentaries have won various awards and have appeared at the Al Jazeera International Documentary Film Festival 2011, Women's Voices Now Film Festival Los Angeles 2011, Bilder vom Film Festival 2008 award, International Film Festival Trevignano 2007, and the International Film Festival Almata 2006.

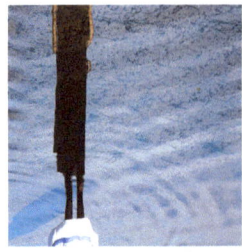
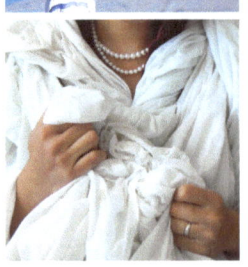

Gazelle Samizay/USA
Left, im/pure & This Will Be the Last
www.gazellesamizay.com

Gazelle Samizay was born in Kabul, Afghanistan, and now resides in Los Angeles. Her photographs and videos have been exhibited across the United States and internationally, including Brazil, Bulgaria, Egypt, France, Indonesia, Pakistan, U.A.E., and the UK. In addition to her studio practice, she has taught in Afghanistan, Jordan, and the US, and her writing has been published in *One Story, Thirty Stories: An Anthology of Contemporary Afghan American Literature*. Samizay is a recipient of the Princess Grace Experimental Film Honoraria, the 1885 Society Graduate Fellowship in Arts and Humanities, and the Northern Trust Enrichment Award, among others. She received her MFA in photography at the University of Arizona and is a photography professor at the Art Institute of Pittsburgh-Online Division. She also serves on the board of the Bo M. Karlsson Foundation, which provides scholarships for Nepali women to attend college.

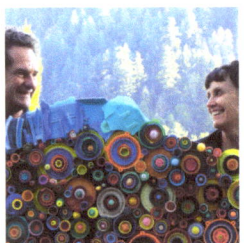

Eric Slatkin & Tess Thackara/USA
One Plastic Beach
ericslatkin.com

Eric Slatkin is an Emmy-nominated, Webby Award-winning filmmaker living in Los Angeles. He is the Creative Director of Content at Tastemade.

Tess Thackara is Editorial Associate at Artsy Inc., and a candidate in the Art History MA program at Hunter College. She has run educational art programs in San Francisco and Miami and contributed writing to New York Magazine, BOMB Magazine, Whitewall, Art Practical, Guernica and SFMOMA's blog Open Space among other publications.

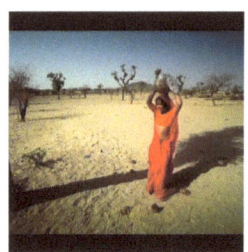

Swarathma/India
Pyaasi (The Thirsty)
www.swarathma.com

Swarathma is a contemporary folk-fusion band based in Bangalore, India. The group represents the sound of today's India: rooted in tradition, yet with sights set firmly on the modern world. The sound is Indian folk and classical with reggae, blues, and jazz in a one-of-a-kind blend. Swarathma released two albums on EMI in 2009, and has worked with the legendary John Leckie (Radiohead, Muse). They swept the 2009 Jack Daniels Indian Rock Awards, winning Band, Song and Album of the Year. The band is known for a visually electric interactive stage act, featuring faux folk-horses and a Nehru Topis. This act won over audiences at top festivals such as Lovebox and Larmer Tree Festivals in London and Awtar Festival in Morocco. Swarathma has also traveled to Hong Kong and Singapore. *Pyaasi*, Swarathma's first music video, was launched in 2010 and funded by the Gibson Foundation and the Global Water Challenge. It tells of the fragility of water through a story of contrasts and features the voice of legendary Indian classical singer Shubha Mudgal. Academy Award-nominated filmmaker Shekhar Kapur was the video's creative consultant. It was shot in the wind-swept arid desert of Rajasthan. Swarathma plays one free show for every paid show, giving back their music to those who may not be able to access it easily. The band performs in leprosy centers, villages, orphanages, and for street kids. With music that is strong and beautiful, contemporary and relevant, hard-hitting and tongue-in-cheek, they're one of India's most sought-after live acts.

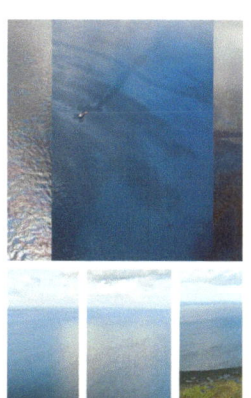

Michel Varisco/USA
Shifting

www.michelvarisco.com

Michel Varisco is a native New Orleans artist and an artist-mentor at New Orleans Center for Creative Arts. She works in photography, assemblage and site-specific installations exploring change, loss, and regeneration. Recent work focuses around the Louisiana Wetlands in a highly lauded series titled *Shifting* and explores the dynamic changes and cycles of loss on the coast of Louisiana from both natural and man-made causes. Varisco's work has been published and shown internationally, and is included in corporate, private, and public collections in the United States and abroad.

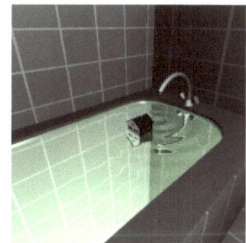

Susanne Wiegner/Germany
Constant Dripping or No Escape

www.susannewiegner.de

Susanne Wiegner studied architecture at the Academy of Fine Arts in Munich and at Pratt Institute in New York City. She now works as an architect and 3-D-artist in Munich, Germany. In addition to projects in real space, for several years she has been creating 3-D computer animations dealing with literature and with virtual space. Her work has been shown at the Pinakothek der Moderne in Munich, the Jenisch Haus in Hamburg, the Art + Technology Center EYEBEAM in New York City, ZKM in Karlsruhe, festivals in Marseille, Rotterdam, Berlin, Athens, Lisbon, Copenhagen, New Delhi, Damascus, Ramallah, Tokyo, London, Buenos Aires, Sao Paulo, Macau, and Vienna. Her film *just midnight* – the adaption of a poem by Robert Lax – won the Film Award, "la parola immaginata 2011," at the Trivigliopoesia Festival in Bergamo and her film *at the museum* won the Ballon-Prize at crosstalk 2012 video art festival, Budapest.

Jennifer Heath
Curator

www.waterwatereverywhere-artshow.com

Jennifer Heath is an independent curator, award-winning cultural journalist, writer, editor, and activist. Her many exhibitions include *The Veil: Visible & Invisible Spaces*, which traveled throughout the United States from 2008 through 2013, *The Art We Love to Hate: Black Velvet*, for which she was named by the Smithsonian as the United States' foremost expert on black velvet painting, and *The Map is Not the Territory: Parallel Paths-Palestinians, Native Americans, Irish*, an exploration of post- and current colonialism, co-curated with Dagmar Painter, which launched in September 2013. Her "locavore" exhibit in 2010, *Resurrections: ECO-logy & ECO-nomy*, invited artists to create functional objects from trash, and featured satellite exhibitions, *Rising Tides: Trashing the Oceans* and *Twilight's Last Gleaming: Nuclear Waste*. She is the author or editor of twelve books of fiction and non-fiction, including *On the Edge of Dream: The Women of Celtic Myth and Legend* (Penguin 1998), *The Echoing Green: The Garden in Myth and Memory* (Penguin 2000), *The Scimitar and the Veil: Extraordinary Women of Islam* (Paulist Press, 2004), *The Veil: Women Writers on its History, Lore, and Politics* and, co-edited with Ashraf Zahedi, *Land of the Unconquerable: The Lives of Contemporary Afghan Women* (both from the University of California Press, 2008 and 2011). *Children of Afghanistan: The Path to Peace,* (with Zahedi) is forthcoming in fall 2014 from the University of Texas Press. Her book *The Jewel and The Ember: Love Stories of the Ancient Middle East* is available at Smashwords E-books Publishers or amazon.com, and extends the tales first explored in a 2001 production with Betsy Tobin's Now or Never Theatre titled *There Was and There Was Not: Wonder Tales of the Islamic World.*

Exhibition Checklist

Evan Abramson and Carmen Elsa Lopez
Carbon for Water
2011
High Definition Video
Sound, 22 minutes

Diane Armitage
The Great River
2002
Digital Video
Sound, 5:02

Ruben Aubrecht
april
2005
MiniDV
Sound, 5:29

Christine Baeumler
Amazon Twilight
2010
Video
Sound, 6:08

Christine Baeumler
Surfacing
2010
Video
Sound, 5:13

Krisanne Baker
Upstream to Downstream (In Our Bloodstreams)
Undated
High Definition Video.
Sound, 2:11

Krisanne Baker
World Water Crises: Potential Effects/Cumulative Effects
Undated
High Definition Video
Sound, 1:52

Manoj Baviskar
I Came... I Saw... Prayed for Someone Whom I Love
2008
MPEG-4
Sound, 8:52

Asa Maria Bengtsson and Ewa Cederstam
FLOW
2006
Video
Sound, 14:06

Beth Block
Leaky Mountain
Undated
1080p Digital
Sound, 9:17

Jaap Blonk
Flabbable 1
2011
Video
Sound, 1:53

Claudia Borgna
Sweep & Weep, Weep & Sweep
2010
High Definition Video
Sound, 10:45

Claudia Borgna
Poise of Tides
2010
High Definition Video
Sound, 5:28

James Brady
Floodland Study #1—visible measures
2009
MiniDV
Sound, 11:40

Fiammetta de Michele
Louisiana
Undated
Video
Sound, 3:42

Jacques del Conte
A Colossal Fracking Mess
2010
Digital Video - NTSC
Sound, 10:08

Robert Ladislas Derr
Conservation of Momentum
2009
High Definition MiniDV
Sound, 2:41

Mary Rachel Fanning
The Trophy
2009
Underwater Surveillance Video Camera
Silent, 8:55

Diego Fiori
*Silenzio: Birth and Death of the Alter Ego
Act II –from Trilogy of SILENCE*
Undated
16mm Film
Sound, 5 minutes

Georgie Friedman
Light of the Storm
2011
High Definition Video
Sound, 2:50

Friends of the Earth Middle East
Good Water Neighbors
2011
High Definition Video
Sound, 14 minutes

J Gluckstern
Ditches of Boulder
2009
Digital Video
Sound, 8:18

J Gluckstern
lyons, co, 10-10-13
2013
16mm Film
Silent, 3 minutes

Henry Gwiazda
there's whispering
2003
Quicktime Movie
Sound, 3:45

Monika Hapsari
Big Trash
2011
Video
Sound, 4:16

Jason Houston
Indonesian Borneo: Water Meditation
2009
DSLR/Digital Video
Sound, 30 seconds

Jason Houston
Indonesian Borneo: Rain Meditation
2009
DSLR/Digital Video
Sound, 30 seconds

Carla Pataky & International Rivers, Inc.
A River Runs Through Us
2010
Video
Sound, 22:30

Basia Irland
A Gathering of Waters: Rio Grande Source to Sea
1999
Video
Sound, 26:30

Basia Irland
Book of Drought: A Water Memory
2009
Video
Sound, 3:38

Robin Johnston
Death of Light in Symmetry
2011
Windows Media Video
Sound, 5:19

Pat Law
Voyage
2010
High Definition Video
Sound, 3:30

Liz Marshall
Excerpt from Water on the Table
2010
High Definition Video
Sound, 6:36

Smriti Mehra
Tade
2010
MiniDV - PAL
Sound, 8 minutes

Patrizia Monzani
found footage
2006
Video/Internet appropriations from opensource films
Sound, 5:12

Jessica Plumb
Climate Change: An Intimate Portrait
Undated
Video
Sound, 2:16

Carolyn Radlo and Alanna Simone
Rice Relief
2009/2011
DSLR/Digital Video
Sound, 2:44

Tobias Rosenberger
Sevastopol in August
Undated
Video
Sound, 5 minutes

Alka Sadat
The Kabul Sea
Undated
High Definition Video
Original Title: دریای کابل
Sound, 3:20

Gazelle Samizay
Left
2011
High Definition Video
Sound, 2:51

Gazelle Samizay
im/pure
2011
High Definition Video
Sound, 2:20

Gazelle Samizay
This Will be the Last
2009
Standard Definition Video
Sound, 5:30

Erik Slatkin and Tess Thackara
One Plastic Beach
2010
High Definition Video
Sound, 7:59

Swarathma
Pyaasi (The Thirsty)
Undated
Film
Sound, 4:05

Michel Varisco
Shifting
2012
Still Photographs and Audio
Sound, 7:12

Susanne Wiegner
Constant Dripping or No Escape
2009
3-D Computer Animation
Sound, 3:20

Resources

National and International Advocacy, Education, and Research Organizations

350.org – www.350.org/en

AEN: Arts & the Environment – www.ciwem.org/arts

American Littoral Society – www.littoralsociety.org

American Rivers – www.americanrivers.org

Amigos Bravos – www.amigosbravos.org

Barataria-Terrebonne National Estuary Program – www.btnep.org/BTNEP/home.aspx

Blue Planet Network – blueplanetnetwork.org

Blue Planet Project – www.blueplanetproject.net

Cape Farewell – www.capefarewell.com

Center for a Livable Future – www.jhsph.edu/research/centers-and-institutes/johns-hopkins-center-for-a-livable-future/index.html

Center for a New American Dream – www.newdream.org

Center for Biological Diversity – www.biologicaldiversity.org

Center for Watershed Protection – www.cwp.org

Charity Navigators – www.charitynavigator.org

Clean Beaches Council – www.cleanbeaches.org

Colorado Ocean Coalition: Creating an Inland Ocean Movement – coloradoocean.org

Concerned Citizens Coalition of Stockton – www.cccos.org

Corporate Accountability International – www.stopcorporateabuse.org

David Suzuki Foundation – www.davidsuzuki.org

Ducks Unlimited – www.ducks.org

Earthjustice: Because the Earth Needs a Good Lawyer – www.earthjustice.org

EarthEcho International – www.earthecho.org

Environmental Investigation Agency – www.eia-international.org

Felton Flow (Friends of Locally Owned Water) – www.feltonflow.org

Food & Water Watch – www.foodandwaterwatch.org

Friends of the Earth – www.foe.org

Friends of the Earth Middle East – www.foeme.org/www/?module=home

Friends of the Everglades – www.everglades.org

Generation Blue (Austria) – www.generationblue.at

Global Water Policy Project – www.globalwaterpolicy.org

Global Water Program (Johns Hopkins University) – globalwater.jhu.edu

A Global Water Story – www.worldviews.net/a-global-water-story

Greenpeace USA – www.greenpeace.org/usa/en

Greenpeace International – www.greenpeace.org/international/en

Gulf Restoration Network – www.healthygulf.org

H2O Conserve Water Calculator – www.h2oconserve.org/home.php?pd=index

Interfaith Center for Corporate Responsibility – www.iccr.org

International Rivers – www.internationalrivers.org

Keepers of the Waters – keepersofthewaters.org/BetsyDamon2012.cfm

Khaled bin Sultan Living Oceans Foundation – www.livingoceansfoundation.org

MAIA Project, Bringing Clean Water to the Children of Palestine – www.mecaforpeace.org/projects/maia-project

Michigan Citizens for Water Conservation – www.savemiwater.org

The Mothers Project, Inc. – www.mothersagainstfracking.com

In Colorado – www.mothersforsustainableenergy.com/environmental-threats/2012/07/19/calling-on-mothers-to-save-colorado-from-hydrofrackingsign-on-now

National Oceanic and Atmospheric Administration (NOAA) Restoration Center – www.habitat.noaa.gov/restoration/index.html

Natural Resources Defense Council – www.nrdc.org

Navdanya: Seed keepers Network Defense Against Biopiracy – www.navdanya.org

New Mexico Acequia Association – www.lasacequias.org

Nora York, "Water, Water Everywhere/Nay Any Drop to Drink" – www.youtube.com/watch?v=dJHuO5cCnIY&feature=c4-overview&list=UUDo3Cb8Gvpaze6XUJ7GrUBA

Oceana – oceana.org/en

The Ocean Conservancy – www.oceanconservancy.org

Pacific Institute – www.pacinst.org

Polaris Institute – www.polarisinstitute.org

Restore America's Estuaries – www.estuaries.org

Riverkeeper: New York's Clean Water Advocate – www.riverkeeper.org

Sea Shepherd Conservation Society – www.seashepherd.org

Sustainable WASH Solutions: A global portal for advancing sustainability in WASH – sustainablewash.org

U.S. Environmental Protection Agency, Office of Wetlands, Oceans, and Watersheds – water.epa.gov/aboutow/owow

The WASH Sustainability Charter – washcharter.org

Water Aid – www.wateraidamerica.org

World Water Council – www.worldwatercouncil.org

Arts, Films, Film Clips and Other Media

Alternative Radio - www.alternativeradio.org
  Maude Barlow: "The Global Water Crisis"
  Maude Barlow: "Peak Water"
  Maude Barlow: "Not a Drop to Drink"
  Deborah Kaufman and Alan Snitow: "The Corporate Takeover of Water"
  Vandana Shiva, Maude Barlow, and Tony Clark: "Liquid Assets: Water for the Highest Bidder"
  Andrew Nikiforuk: "Tar Sands: Canada's Mordor"
  Najma Sadeque: "Pakistan: Environment in Crisis"
  Barbara Bernstein: "Rivers That Were"
  Lester Brown: "Plan B: A Blueprint for People & the Planet"
  David Suzuki: "Betraying Nature"

Alternet, "Top Ten Water Trailblazers" – www.trust.org/alertnet/news/top-10-water-trailblazers
  Manoranjan Mondal; Gemma Bulos; Anupam Mishra; Asit Biswas; Ma Tsepo Khumbane; Rajendra Singh; Margaret Nakato; Andrew Benedek; Diana Iskreva; Ned Breslin

American Museum of Natural History-Water: H2O=Life – www.amnh.org/exhibitions/water

Chris Jordan: "Midway-Message from the Gyre" – www.chrisjordan.com/gallery/midway/#CF000313%2018x24

Cultura21 Network – www.cultura21.net

Betsy Damon, Keepers of the Waters – keepersofthewaters.org/BetsyDamon2012.cfm

EcoArts Connections – www.ecoartsonline.org

Ecoartnetwork – www.ecoartnetwork.org

En cuánto tiempo se derrite un cubito? (2010), a short play by renowned Argentinian playwright Alejandro Finzi – www.marcelolirio.com.ar/noticias/?p=30

"Gasland: A Film by Josh Fox," www.gaslandthemovie.com

Green Museum – www.greenmuseum.org

Image2020: Art and Climate Change – www.imagine2020.eu

Immersion Emergencies – www.immersion-emergencies.ca

Nigel Dunnett, "The London Olympic Park Swales and Rain Gardens" – www.nigeldunnett.info/Londonolympicpark/styled/Olympicparksustainable%20drainage.html

Occidental Arts and Ecology Water Institute – www.oaec.org/water-institute

"Ocean Frontiers," www.facebook.com/events/151847808283021

"Pirate for the Sea" – www.seashepherd.org

River of Words: Center for Environmental Literacy – www.stmarys-ca.edu/center-for-environmental-literacy/river-of-words

"Thirst," Snitow-Kaufman Productions, www.snitow-kaufman.org

"Water Lilies," by Judith Selby Lang – www.youtube.com/watch?v=KC23NnCghLk

Women Environmental Artist Directory (WEAD) – www.weadartists.org

A Brief Bibliography

Atchafalaya Houseboat: My Years in the Louisiana Swamp, Gwen Roland, C. C. Lockwood (Photographer), Louisiana State University Press, 2006

The Atlas of Water, Second Edition: Mapping the World's Most Critical Resource, Maggie Black, Jannet King, University of California Press, 2009

Bayou Farewell: The Rich Life and Tragic Death of Louisiana's Cajun Coast, Mike Tidwell, Vintage, 2004

The Big Thirst, The Secret Life and Turbulent Future of Water, Charles Fishman, Free Press, 2011

Cadillac Desert: The American West and Its Disappearing Water, Marc Reisner, Penguin, 1993

Conservation Refugees: The Hundred-Year Conflict Between Global Conservation and Native Peoples, Mark Dowie, MIT Press, 2009

A Ditch in Time: The City, the West and Water, Patricia Nelson Limerick, Fulcrum Publishing, 2012

Drinking Water, James Salzman, Overlook Press, 2012

Life on the Mississippi, Mark Twain, Dover Publications, 2000

50 Ways to Save the Ocean, David Helvarg, New World Library, 2006

The Ripple Effect: The Fate of Fresh Water in the Twenty-first Century, Alex Prud'homme, Scribner, 2011

Rising Tide: The Great Mississippi Flood of 1927 and How it Changed America, John M. Barry, Simon and Schuster, 1998

A River and Its City: The Nature of Landscape in New Orleans, Ari Kelman, University of California Press, 2006

Silent Spring, Rachel Carson, Houghton Mifflin Company, 2002

Taking on Water: How One Water Expert Challenged her Inner Hypocrite, Reduced her Water Footprint (without Sacrificing a Toasty Shower), and Found Nirvana, Wendy J. Pabich, Water Futures, Inc., 2012

Tar Sands: Dirty Oil and the Future of a Continent, Andrew Nikiforuk, Greystone Books, 2010

Thirst: Water and Power in the Ancient World, Steven Mithen, Harvard University Press, 2012

Tropic of Chaos: Climate Change and the New Geography of Violence, Christian Parenti, Nation Books, 2011

Under the Surface: Fracking, Fortunes, and the Fate of the Marcellus Shale, Tom Wilber, Cornell University Press, 2012

Water Consciousness, How We All Have To Change To Protect Our Most Critical Resource, Tara Lohan, Alternet Books, 2008

Water: The Epic Struggle for Wealth, Power, and Civilization, Steven Solomon, Harper Perennial, 2011

Water Wars: Privatization, Pollution, and Profit, Vandana Shiva, South End Press, 2002

When Rivers Run Dry: Water – The Defining Crisis of the Twenty-first Century, Fred Pearce, Beacon Press, 2007

World on the Edge: How to Prevent Environmental and Economic Collapse, Lester R. Brown, W.W. Norton & Company, 2011

Water, Water Everywhere: Paean to a Vanishing Resource

a touring new media art exhibition

waterwatereverywhere-artshow.com

A writing exercise for kids

QUESTIONS ABOUT WATER?

As you explore *Water, Water Everywhere* and contemplate the artworks, consider these questions created by poet Jack Collom for a "River of Words" project* with students. If you have a writing implement (pen, paper, phone notepad…), you might jot down your ideas following this set of suggested thinking points. If you are a teacher, these questions can open up a flow in the classroom:

- What do different kinds of water feel like?

- Name some sounds water makes.

- What does water taste like?

- What does rippling water look like?

- Have you ever been afraid of water?

- Is water alive? (Discuss.)

- Can you write a letter to water?

Drawing by Kate P. Heath, 2014

- Does water think and dream? About what?

- What do water and ice and fog say to each other? (Write a dialogue.)

- What does a drop of water want?

- What happens in water heaven?

- Does water have colors? What happens to them?

- How can we hurt water?

- What would a world without water be like?

Jack Collom is a poet whose focus is primarily on the ecology. He teaches Ecology Literature at Naropa University and is a poet in residence in primary and secondary schools. He is the author of Poetry Everywhere: Teaching Poetry and Writing in the School and the Community, Red Car Goes By, *and* Second Nature, *among others. "River of Words" is a program of The Center for Environmental Literacy and a part of the Kalmanovitz School of Education at St. Mary's College of California.*

Drawing by Kate P. Heath, 2014

May 2014

flow ...

W hy don't we   just ripple, drip,

A   dmit

T   hat water is the very kiss of a living (this)

E   xistence, yet we've been wrecking, killing it (us), so now let's strive and re-strive to

R ectify the   liquid situation?

—Jack Collom

www.ingramcontent.com/pod-product-compliance
Lightning Source LLC
Chambersburg PA
CBHW051155220526
45473CB00003B/779